Men Are ▶
Slobs
Women Are
◀ Neat

KIMBERLY ALYN
& BOB PHILLIPS

HARVEST HOUSE PUBLISHERS

EUGENE, OREGON

Cover by Dugan Design Group, Bloomington, Minnesota

Cover illustration © Dugan Design Group

MEN ARE SLOBS, WOMEN ARE NEAT
Copyright © 2010 by Kimberly Alyn and Bob Phillips
Published by Harvest House Publishers
Eugene, Oregon 97402
www.harvesthousepublishers.com

Library of Congress Cataloging-in-Publication Data
Alyn, Kimberly
Men are slobs, women are neat / Kimberly Alyn and Bob Phillips.
   p. cm.
Includes bibliographical references.
ISBN 978-0-7369-2669-0 (pbk.)
1. Sex differences. 2. Sex role. 3. Stereotypes (Social psychology) 4. Interpersonal relations.
5. Man-woman relationships. I. Phillips, Bob II. Title.
HQ1075.A445 2010
155.3'3—dc22

            2009017190

Printed in the United States of America

10 11 12 13 14 15 16 17 18 / VP-SK / 10 9 8 7 6 5 4 3 2 1

Acknowledgments

Thank you to Tiffany Donovan for your proofing and editing. (Tiffany, you have a keen eye!) Thank you to Brianna Donovan for your formatting assistance and extra support during this project. A special thank you to Rena Rosenzveig and Nikkita Edmond for all of your hard work doing research for this book.

We would also like to thank all of our loved ones, who have supported us in this project and the many other projects we both participate in. God has truly blessed us with amazing families and friends. May He bless all of you abundantly in all that you do.

Contents

A Note from the Authors

This book was written by two friends who have spent many years speaking, teaching, and consulting with individuals, organizations, and businesses. We wrote the chapters together and agree about the thoughts they contain, so we usually use the first-person singular when referring to ourselves.

Most of the illustrations are also in the first person singular because they record what actually happened to either Bob or Kim. We felt that a first-person account of real-life events would present the material most powerfully and help you sense what really happened. We have not identified who is speaking and have changed people's names to protect their privacy.

Kimberly Alyn and Bob Phillips

Let's Start with the Truth

Mark Twain once said, "The striking difference between a cat and a lie is that a cat only has nine lives." When it comes to the gender differences between men and women, we have been told lie after lie.

These gender distortions have been expressed so loud and so long that many people assume they are true. They have been passed along like urban legends. But common sense tells us that many of these gender distinctions are just that—legends.

Plenty of studies have confirmed that we live in a society of gender stereotypes. When people pass along these myths and other people believe them, they can seriously damage relationships. Folks who retell these faulty concepts may be well-meaning, but they actually confuse and mislead people and hurt themselves.

Some experts attribute the differences between men and women to situations or events in their lives rather than their gender. Others say that the differences are culturally constructed. But some people continue to hold to the traditional gender lies we address in this book.

Of course, men and women really are different, and that is good and great. *Viva* the differences! Our purpose in writing is not to elevate one gender over the other or to address a politically correct agenda. We will keep men and women on an equal playing field.

Our approach is to suggest that the differences between men and women have more to do with social style than with gender. Let's begin by defining a few terms:

- *Social style*: your natural inclinations inherited at birth, sometimes called your temperament.

- *Personality*: the way you individually express your inherited social style. This can be affected or influenced by your family, your culture, and your environment.

- *Character*: the quality of your individual personality. This is influenced by your personal morals, values, and ethics.

The understanding of social styles is perhaps one of the greatest tools for creating more cohesive relationships. It can unify husbands and wives, produce harmony in families, and make the workplace environment more enjoyable.

It is time to do some myth busting and set the record straight on a few things. Let's identify some untrue gender stereotypes and bury them in the graveyard of erroneous facts. We can shine the light of truth on some old wives' tales.

A Look at Real Life

When Dave came home from work, he was completely frustrated with his day. Even after he'd been home a few hours, he carried the pain of a difficult interaction with his boss. He looked over at his wife, who was typing frantically at the computer. He wanted so desperately to just feel her warm and safe arms around him as he shared his hurt, but something inside of him cautioned against it. *She might think I'm a sissy. Real men suck it up and deal with it. Stop being weak and take it like a man, Dave!* He sighed deeply and retreated to the den to unwind.

Angela glanced up as he walked past her. She sensed his tense demeanor and knew something was wrong. She looked back at the computer screen and took a deep breath. *I really need to get this finished. Maybe Dave just needs some time alone. I suppose women are supposed to be sensitive and intuitive, but I don't feel that way right now. What's wrong with me? Get your butt up, Angela, and go see if he needs anything.* As she poked her head into the den, Dave had his nose in the newspaper. Angela cleared her throat slightly and asked, "Honey, is everything okay? Is there anything you want to talk about?"

Dave glanced up and politely answered, "No, I just had a long day. I'll be out in a few minutes." Angela smiled and headed back to her computer.

Dave and Angela, like millions of others, are victims of the gender lies they have been fed throughout their lives. They feel pulled in directions that run counter to gender stereotypes, and they are both too afraid to admit it.

This book will dispel many lies, myths, and urban legends that exist about gender differences. It will challenge many of the gender stereotypes you have come to believe. Yes, many gender differences are valid (most of which are obvious), and we will look at some of those as well. But we will spend most of our time considering the gender lies you've been fed.

Alleged experts have told people for many years that men are thinkers and women are feelers. They claim that women like to talk things out and men like to withdraw, and they affirm that women get their sense of self through relationships while men get their sense of self through accomplishments. But when these experts meet people who say, "Wait a minute, my husband is the one who likes to talk, and I'm the one who like to get projects done," the experts respond by saying, "Well, you're experiencing a role reversal, and that's normal." They may even go on to try to convince people why this role reversal took place. Maybe the woman is becoming more assertive and less emotional because she has taken on a new role of working outside the home. Maybe the man is becoming more feminine and sensitive because he is forced to take on some roles that a woman would normally have. *Hogwash!*

The scrutiny of human nature on a small scale is one of the most dangerous of employments; the study of it on a large scale is one of the safest and truest.

—Isaac Taylor

The divorce rate in America is still at 40 to 50 percent (depending on which research firm you ask), and people are still struggling with relationships whether they are married, dating, or just friends. If people's relational problems were simply gender-based, all women would get along with other women because they understand each other. All men would get along by simply grunting at each other, watching television, and bonding. But everyone has relationship and conflict problems with a wide variety of people, regardless of gender. Unfortunately, gender myths are keeping people from truly understanding each other.

Before I address some of the lies one by one, let me explain the basis of my theory. I have conducted many of my own studies and interviews and read many other studies and testimonies, but I rest my case on the science of common sense and behavior observation, as you will discover for yourself.

Here is my conclusion: The differences that exist between people are results of social style variances and not gender. Unfortunately, many well-intended but misguided experts have led us to believe that men have certain characteristics and women have the exact opposite. Again, some of those differences are actually true, and the ones that are true are often the ones that people don't like and may even dismiss as false. On the other hand, the mythical fabrications that have been passed around for years are the ones people tend to embrace and perpetuate. Crazy, isn't it?

As a result, men and women find themselves scrambling to figure each other out. In case you haven't noticed, it's not working. One of the reasons it's not working is that we have been fed inaccurate information that can lead to relationship frustration and even identity crises. Men are told they are built a certain way just because they are male. When they find themselves instinctively acting differently from the stereotypical male, they may become confused and afraid to tell anyone. Many women feel like outsiders in some women's groups because they don't fit the mold either. They would rather hang around with men than with women.

The lightbulb is about to come on. As you make your way through this book, things will finally start to make sense. You'll get answers to some confusing relationship questions. You'll discover why so many people in your life do not fit the gender stereotypes.

I teach seminars on this topic, and thousands of people have watched the light come on in their own lives. They have come to me and said things like this: "*Wow*—this makes so much sense! I thought my husband was weird because he was so emotional and needy and I wasn't. And I thought I was weird because I didn't feel the need to get on the phone with my girlfriends every time I had a fight with my husband. This makes sense."

Men have told me, "I wish I had heard this information years ago. I have never felt normal because of what everyone says about men and women. I don't want to retreat when I get home from work—I want to talk to my wife or my friends. I want to experience romance and share my feelings and not feel as if that makes me less of a man. I am so sick of everyone saying that men are practical and women are romantic. I am much more romantic than my wife is."

Of course, some experts would just tell him he was experiencing a role reversal or he was the exception instead of telling him the truth: He was born that way, and a million other men out there are just like him.

The Truth Starts Here

Before I start pounding away at some lies, let me first tell you the truth. This will explain why I make statements like "Women *do not* talk more than men."

Many of the differences we attribute to gender are actually attributable to social style, or temperament. There are four basic types of people in the world, and yes, you are one of them. We wrote an entire book about social styles called *How to Deal with Annoying People*. Social style analysis has been an area of interest and expertise for both of us over the past 20 years. The overview of each style that follows will help you understand why people are the way they are.

As you read through the descriptions of the four social styles, make a mental note of which one describes you best. Then as you read the rest of the book, you'll be thinking, *Aha...that's why I'm that way!* (You can also turn to appendix A and find a reference chart that will show you how to find your social style very quickly and a section that covers each style in more detail.)

Spouting off before listening to the facts is both shameful and foolish...The first to speak in court sounds right—until the cross-examination begins.
—Proverbs 18:13,17

Social Styles

Analyticals. People with this social style are introverted and task oriented. They like to think through their decisions and analyze everything. They are neat, clean, organized, loyal, and self-disciplined, and they like to do things right the first time.

But these folks can also be moody, critical, and indecisive. They hate conflict, and they tend to be antisocial because they are not very outgoing and they focus on getting tasks completed. Some famous Analytical people are Spock from *Star Trek*, Agatha Christy, Bill Gates, Thomas Edison, and Marie Curie (physicist and chemist).

Drivers. Drivers are type-A, natural-born leaders. They too are task-oriented, but unlike Analyticals, they are extroverts. They are determined, productive, and decisive. They are visionaries who get a lot of stuff done.

But Drivers can also be unsympathetic, insensitive, and proud. They are not the most warm and fuzzy people you'll meet. They can be sarcastic and have little patience for perceived incompetence. Theodore Roosevelt, Hilary Clinton, Donald Trump, and the cartoon character Lucy from *Peanuts* are classic Drivers.

Amiables. Amiables are introverted like Analyticals, but they are relationship oriented, not task oriented. They are easygoing and likeable, partly because they avoid conflict whenever they can. They are inoffensive, diplomatic, and calm. They are often sympathetic and giving.

But Amiables can also be indecisive, apathetic, and noncommunicative. They make great listeners but don't always like to share what's on their mind. They tend to be lax on discipline with their children or with workers whom they supervise. Mother Theresa, Jimmy Carter, Princess Diana, and the cartoon character Charlie Brown are famous Amiables.

Expressives. This is the easiest social style to identify because Expressives are extroverts and relationship oriented. You can see and hear them coming! They are usually the life of the party and like to have a good time. They are charismatic, enthusiastic, and ambitious. They love to talk with just about anyone.

But Expressives can be reactive, obnoxious, loud, and disorganized. They tend to exaggerate and enjoy being the center of attention. They chafe under structure and rules and can get themselves into trouble because of that. Jim Carey, Rosie O'Donnell, Bill Clinton, and Lucille Ball are clearly Expressives.

Why You Need to Know This

These social styles determine behavior much more than gender does. As we consider some gender myths and urban legends, we will replace those lies with the truth about social styles. Along the way, I'll give you even more information about each social style. As a result, you will understand more about people and their real needs, and you'll be able to make some helpful adjustments in your relationships.

The concept of social styles originated with Hypocrites back in 400 BC. He described four basic temperaments: melancholy (the Analytical), choleric (the Driver), phlegmatic (the Amiable), and sanguine (the Expressive). He asserted that the elements inside the body (phlegm, blood, and bile) helped determine the personality, and those elements were inherited (which explains why some kids are like Mom and some are like Dad).

You don't have to look too far to see why you are the way you are. I heard a woman say once, "Well, I tend to be assertive and stubborn because I watched my dad walk all over my mom and she just took it and never said a word. Because of that, I learned to stand up for myself." A more accurate explanation would be that Dad was a Driver and Mom was an Amiable, and the daughter turned out to be a Driver like Dad. She had tendencies toward assertiveness from the day she was born.

Nothing is more difficult than competing with a myth.
—Françoise Giroud

I have heard people use the same type of story with a reverse argument: "I tend to avoid conflict because my dad was overbearing and my mom was withdrawn and never did anything about it. So I learned to just avoid conflict and try not to deal with it." In this case, the daughter turned out to be an Amiable, like her mom. The environment didn't dictate her disposition; her inherent social style did.

You don't get to choose your social style—you are born with it. Sorry, that's the way it is. And it's not based on the birth order in your family either. You may end up modifying it to some degree based on your culture or upbringing, but you can't decide that you will be a Driver if you were born an Amiable. You can choose behavior, which means you can decide to *act* like an Amiable, but you'll still be a Driver. You might try to be nicer to people and exercise more patience, but when someone drives too slowly in front of you, your natural instinct will still be to feel some level of impatience. You may not act on that impatience and may instead choose the behavior of patience, but you'll still be a Driver who needs to grow in that area.

So your gender doesn't dictate most of your responses (and I say *most* because some are in fact results of gender); your social style does. People have asked me whether I believe culture or environment plays a role in human behavior and response tendency. I do not believe that the environment forms your social style, but I do believe it affects the way you manifest your social style through your personality.

For example, in many cultures and religions, women are prohibited to teach, speak, or lead. As a result, many women would appear to be shy and withdrawn followers. That is not necessarily the case. A woman may have an assertive social style (a Driver or an Expressive), but she may choose a different behavior as a willful (or forced) submission to her culture or religion. She may not have the right to vote in certain countries, but that doesn't mean she doesn't have an internal drive or a desire to be more assertive even though she must stifle that drive.

Maybe you've heard the story of the strong-willed little boy who kept standing on the pew in church. His mother pulled him down and told him to sit still and be quiet. He continued to stand up until she finally pulled him close enough to her to whisper in his ear, "If you get up one more time, you'll get a strong swat to your behind when we get home!" The boy gave in and sat on the pew with his arms crossed and his teeth gritted. He glared up at his mother and said, "I'm sitting down on the outside, but I'm standing up on the inside!"

Men and women may succumb to gender stereotypes and cultural roles, but that does not mean they are expressing who they really are. A man may very well be unemotional on the outside (for the world to see) but experience a great deal of emotion on the inside (that he hides). A woman may fulfill an obligation to her friends by going shopping but feel as if she's going crazy watching them take forever to decide which pair of shoes to buy.

We are easily influenced as a society. We succumb to fear, peer pressure, and mob thinking. If society tells us that real men don't cry, men who are born with a natural disposition to emotion (Amiables and Expressives) may condition themselves to stuff their emotions. If society tells us that women aren't as well suited for leadership roles as men, some women may never pursue positions they could have excelled at.

As we delve into the gender lies, ask yourself if you have fallen victim to these myths and how they might be affecting you and your relationships. Once you come to a deeper understanding of who you really are, you'll be free to throw off the cloak of stereotypes and wrap yourself in the truth of who God created you to be.

Common Sense

As we dissect these gender myths, try to clear your mind of the stereotypes you've been fed. Once you set those aside, you can objectively evaluate yourself and others around you. You may find that some gender stereotypes actually fit you (maybe you're a woman who likes to talk a lot). If that's the case, I will show you how that is mostly attributable to your social style, not your gender. As you begin to apply common sense with behavior observation, you will discover that many of your male friends and associates like to talk just as much as you do. That's because they have the same social style as you, not because they are the same gender or the opposite gender.

If you're a man and you get a lot of self-fulfillment out of accomplishing things, you may think you fit the gender mold. But you'll see why that is more attributable to your inherited social style. As you start to observe behavior around you and dismiss gender myths, you'll notice something. Many of your female friends and associates also get a tremendous amount of self-fulfillment out of accomplishing tasks or progressing in their careers. That's because these women have the same social style you do.

When you set aside your preconditioned ideas about gender, your common sense will kick in and you can start to clearly observe normal behavior in others. You'll see for yourself that these gender myths just don't fit everyone, whereas the social style theory does.

I challenge you as you read this book to rethink your views on gender stereotypes. I am confident you will discover what I have discovered: We have been fed gender lies most of our lives.

Part 1:

The Ten Most Common
(and Damaging) Gender Lies

1

Women Talk, Men Don't

This is the biggest, most commonly accepted, and most widely spread gender lie. That's why I'm addressing it first and spending some time to dispel this mindless myth.

First of all, why has this become such an accepted stereotype? To begin with, when we hear something often enough, we start to believe it. Think about all the things you heard and believed as a kid (and maybe still do). "If you swallow gum, it will take years to come out." Not true. It comes out like any other indigestible item you swallow. "Sitting too close to the television or watching television in the dark will damage your eyes." Not true. Your eyes may feel some strain, but it certainly won't damage them. "Cracking your knuckles causes arthritis." This is also not true. Parents just made it up so they wouldn't have to hear that irritating sound of your fingers popping.

Nearly every child has had to endure this myth: "You have to wait an hour after eating to go swimming or you could cramp up and drown." Not true. There is no danger in swimming after you eat unless you don't know how to swim. Then you would probably drown.

They say women talk too much. If you
have worked in Congress you know that
the filibuster was invented by men.
—Clare Booth Luce

I am truly amazed at how gullible we are as a society. The Internet provides ample proof. I constantly get trash in my inbox box about how the postal service is going to start taxing e-mails to make up for lost revenue on snail mail. They go on to suggest that I need to put my name at the bottom of the e-mail and pass it on to stop some horrible and pending legislation. Most people don't even bother to check the veracity of these messages before they forward them on to their entire address book. Myths, legends, and folklore—that's all most of these messages are. (By the way, you can stop spreading lies by checking the validity of many urban legends at www.Snopes.com.)

When a rumor, legend, or tall tale spreads enough, we come to accept it. This is how we have come to accept the blatant lie that women talk more than men. Some well-known experts continue to quote statistics that are not backed by actual studies. Some experts claim that women talk a staggering 20,000 words per day while men eke out a mere 7000. Yet no actual study backs up this ludicrous claim. Other experts have claimed that women use 7000 words per day and men use 2000. Still another expert has said women use 25,000 words per day and men only 12,000. One expert has even attributed women with 50,000 words per day and men with only 25,000. So which is it, folks? None of the above. As it turns out, every time I try to substantiate these numbers, I find something interesting. None of the experts using the numbers have conducted studies counting the number of words used by men and women, nor do they cite anyone who has actually counted the number.

This is not to say that no one has studied how much women and men talk. Two Canadian researchers (Deborah James and Janice Drakich) studied this very topic and reviewed the literature available. They discovered that men and women talk about the same amount (although the amount may vary with the cultural or social setting).

In July of 2007, 345 students at the University of Texas were strapped with recording devices. Researchers found that both men and women spoke about 16,000 words per day. This was an average; three people in the study spoke more than 47,000 words per day, and all three were men. But the student who averaged the lowest (only 700 words per day) was also a man. Gender doesn't dictate how much someone talks.

Think about this for a minute: If we had put Joan Rivers and Gerald Ford in a room together, who would talk more? I think most people would agree that it would be Joan Rivers. Aha! So that proves it—women talk more than men. Not so fast…Joan Rivers would talk more because she is an Expressive, not because she's a woman. Gerald Ford would talk less because he was an Amiable, not because he was a man.

What if we had put Princess Dianna in a room with Robin Williams? Who would talk more? It doesn't take a rocket scientist to figure out that Robin Williams, an Expressive, would talk much more. Gender doesn't dictate how much someone talks; social style does.

If we had put Jerry Lewis in a room with Mother Theresa, Jerry would have done most of the talking because he's Expressive. If we put Ronald Reagan in a room with Jackie Kennedy Onassis, Reagan would also talk more because he was an Expressive.

I believe in an open mind, but not so
open that your brains fall out.

—Arthur Hays Sulzberger

If we had put Richard Nixon in a room with Nicole Kidman, Nixon would have won the talking contest because he was a Driver. Drivers tend to dominate conversations, as do Expressives. The difference is usually what they talk about and their style. Expressives are more relationship oriented, so they tend to talk more about people and fun topics. They use a lot of humor, tell a lot of stories, and tend to be more demonstrative in their gestures. Drivers are more task-oriented, so they tend to talk about more serious subjects and like to debate people on controversial issues. They will make intense eye contact with people and don't have a problem saying what they think.

Amiables and Analyticals, on the other hand, do not like conflict. As a result, they tend to withhold their opinions in order to lessen the tension in a conversation. They are more reserved, so they don't need to talk as much as Drivers and Expressives. Amiables are relationship oriented, so they like to talk about people: friends, relationships, and family. Analyticals like to analyze topics and conversations.

Expressives and Drivers will dominate most conversations while Amiables and Analyticals yield the floor. Their gender doesn't matter. Actually, they are just a microcosm of society in general. Some men are Expressives, some are Drivers, some are Amiables, and some are Analyticals. Just look into your own family and circle of friends. Then identify social style, not gender. You'll discover that your Driver and Expressive friends or family members do most of the talking, regardless of gender.

Who's the Talker?

Let me give you a real-life example of a couple. Josh is an Expressive, and Bri is an Analytical. Experts would tell us that women talk more than men, so Bri should be the talker of the two. But Josh has been talking nonstop since he learned how to say "Da-da." He's been an Expressive since the day he was born, and if no one is around to talk to, he'll talk to himself.

Bri, on the other hand, is an Analytical and will let Josh do most of the talking. When they are out with a group of friends, she tends to be shier and lets him be the center of attention. This has nothing to do with their genders and everything to do with their social styles.

Some people may retort, "Well, those two are exceptions and anomalies, not the rule." This is not the case. Thousands and thousands of other couples are just like Josh and Bri. My research, interviews, and studies have confirmed this, and if you start taking the time to observe behavior in others, you will notice the same thing.

Survey Says

I conducted an online and in-person survey that produced 422 responses. I asked respondents to answer questions that helped me identify their social style. I also asked questions that helped determine characteristics that might be attributable to gender and others that might be attributable to social style. The survey is just one of the tools I used to confirm my assertion that many of the behaviors we attribute to gender are actually attributable to social style. I have also conducted interviews with a wide range of people, and I'll share some of those throughout the book.

We don't see things as they are. We see them as we are.

—Anais Nin

On the survey, I asked the respondents to choose between the two following statements: "I don't talk a lot" and "I tend to talk a lot." I also asked, "In your closest relationship with someone of the opposite sex, who does more of the talking, you or the other person?" (I also gave the option to select "We talk about the same amount of time.") The results did not come as any surprise to me, but I do think they will surprise the experts who contend that women talk more than men.

More men than women selected the options "I talk a lot" or "I talk more." So if we left the study at that, we could just conclude that men talk more than women. But that would be an incomplete evaluation of the real truth. When we look deeper and account for social style, we notice that more Drivers and Expressives filled out the survey than Amiables and Analyticals. Additionally, more male Drivers and Expressives responded than female Drivers and Expressives. This would logically account for the fact that more men said they talked more, because Drivers and Expressives talk more than Amiables and Analyticals.

When we dissect the responses further, we see that nearly all of the men who said they talked more were Drivers or Expressives. The same applied to the women. The men and women who said they talked less in the relationship turned out to be Analyticals or Amiables, just as I anticipated. So the amount of talking in a relationship was not attributable to gender at all; it was attributable to social style.

Gender Lies Can Hurt

Why is this so important? Here's why: Men and women read books about how to make each other happy and speak each other's so-called gender languages, but the books do more harm than good.

You meet someone and you're sure you were lovers in a past life. After two weeks with them, you realize why you haven't kept in touch for the last two thousand years.

—Al Cleathen

I interviewed a couple who explained how gender lies had hurt their relationship. When David fell in love with Karen, he bought her flowers, wrote her poems, and called her often. He read plenty of books that told him women felt loved when men talked to them and let them share their feelings. David started to get a little put off when Karen seemed busy and distracted and didn't want to talk for very long on the phone. He had read that women get their identity from relationships, so he wanted to make himself available to her as often as he could. Besides, he considered himself to be relationship oriented and romantic. He knew he wasn't the stereotypical guy, so doing the things he thought all women wanted was natural for him.

He stopped by Karen's house with a sweet card. Karen was in the middle of a project and was a little put off that David came by unannounced. She had a lot of things to get done and didn't have time to socialize right then. She thanked him and let him know she appreciated it, but she was a little abrupt with him. David left her house feeling hurt and confused. He actually liked to talk and socialize, and he was convinced all women did too.

The myth: Men want to solve their problems alone; women want to talk about their problems.

The truth: Driver and Analytical men and women want to solve their problems alone; Expressive and Amiable men and women want to talk about their problems.

So why didn't Karen seem to appreciate his efforts?

David failed to understand that Karen, like many women, did not fit the gender stereotype because her identity wasn't rooted in relationships. She didn't fit the stereotype of wanting to spend hours talking to her boyfriend. Some experts may have consoled David with the "exception to the rule" excuse or dismissed Karen's behavior as abnormal. Or they may have even speculated that her cold and distant father caused her to put people at a distance.

If only David had understood social style. He would have known that Karen is a Driver, and she hates talking on the phone for very long periods of time. She wants people to get to the point quickly. She focuses on tasks and isn't a needy person. In fact, she's very independent. She viewed David as being too needy and started to become turned off by his approach. Because David was buying into all of the gender myths and didn't understand Karen's social style, he was making matters worse, not better.

Had David known about social style and really done his homework on how to relate to a Driver, he would have known that some of his actions would irritate Karen. Had he not been fed all of the gender lies, he would have known that a Driver (male or female) who is in task mode does not appreciate wasting time on the phone with chitchat. David could have adapted his behavior to meet Karen's needs instead of trying to apply the recommendations that have resulted from gender stereotyping.

Women Talk About Relationships; Men Go in the Cave

Let's look at another myth that relates to women who talk and men who are silent.

In modern Western culture, men often feel accused of being feminine if they want to talk about their problems or share their feelings. Women who don't want to talk about things are accused of using the silent treatment to manipulate men. So women are accused of talking all the time, but they are also accused of using the silent treatment all the time...well, which is it? You can't have it both ways.

In my survey, I asked respondents to make one of the following choices: I prefer to...

A. Talk about and work through my relationship issues.

B. Keep my issues to myself.

According to the widespread gender myths, most of the men should have selected *B*, and most of the women should have selected *A*. Many experts tell us that women want to talk to their girlfriends about their relationships and men would rather retreat into their caves and be left alone. But my own research, interviews, and behavior observation has not shown this to be true.

Drivers and Analyticals are more task oriented than relationship oriented, so they tend to want to work on things themselves. They don't particularly like to chitchat with people about their problems because they would rather spend their time completing projects. Drivers and Analyticals deal with relationships issues by diving into work.

Two great talkers will not travel far together.

—Spanish proverb

Even though Drivers prefer to deal with issues themselves, they are not afraid to talk about issues and problems because they are extroverts. They don't mind conflict, and they will deal with issues that need to be dealt with. They just don't feel the need to focus on what they perceive as small and inconsequential relationship issues when bigger projects need to get done. Drivers and Analyticals will turn to tasks to cope with relationship overload. Amiables and Expressives will turn to relationships to deal with task overload.

Even though Amiables want to work things out and keep peace in relationships, they will clam up to avoid conflict. They don't like conflict, and they will simply give in and agree with other people to avoid it. They prefer to let everyone just get along, and they do what they think is necessary to keep the peace. Sometimes that involves not bringing up a frustrating issue.

Plenty of men like to talk about their problems. Sometimes they perceive this as soft or girly or socially unacceptable. But that doesn't mean they don't want to. Other guys will talk about their relationship issues regardless of what people think.

Construction Workers in the Hen House

Television shows, movies, and books often depict groups of women gathering around to gossip about their relationships. The unflattering term *henhouse* comes to mind. Yet many men do the same thing. I was sitting in my office one day, writing. I had an air conditioning unit sticking out of the window, which allowed for most of the external sounds to travel into my office with ease.

On this particular day, an all-male construction crew was outside my window, working on the building right next to mine. (These guys were about as "manly" as they could be.) As I was attempting to type, I could hear their conversation perfectly.

> Worker one: "Dude, what happened with Cindy? You didn't show up with her at Dan's party Saturday. Are you guys fighting again?"
>
> Worker two: "Actually, she dumped me."
>
> Worker three: "Ouch, Dog! What happened?"
>
> Worker two: "She said I was being too clingy and jealous."
>
> Worker one: "I told you that would happen. You just smother her too much, man."
>
> Worker two: "I was just trying to show her I cared. What was I supposed to do?"
>
> Worker three: "Well, you could have called her a little less or not returned her calls. That's when women come running after you—when they think you don't want them anymore."

Worker two: "I'm just not into all those head games. I am who I am, and if she can't accept me for that, we're just not meant to be."

Worker one: "There are other fish in the sea. In fact, my cousin has been wanting to go out with you for months. I'll invite her to the Downtown Street Fair with us Thursday if you want."

Worker two: "I'm not ready for that yet. I'm still getting over Cindy."

I sat at my computer laughing—not at the unfortunate fellow's situation, but at the way these men were expressing themselves. According to the experts, this should have been a group of women. Instead, it was a group of Expressive and/or Amiable men who wanted to talk about their relationships. Exchanges like this happen everywhere, regardless of what the experts say. And they would occur a lot more often if our culture didn't make Expressive and Amiable men feel as if they were abnormal. Gender lies have made men feel weird if they don't want to retreat to their cave, grunt, and stuff their feelings.

Truth is tough. It will not break, like a bubble,
at a touch. Nay, you may kick it about all day,
and it will be round and full at evening.
—Oliver Wendell Holmes

Before the sitcom *Friends* (the most popular sitcom in history) went off the air, an episode depicted the stereotypical gender myth that women like to talk about the details of relationships and men don't. Ross and Rachel had shared their first kiss. The first scene after the kiss shows all the women gathered in Monica's apartment. Phoebe grabs a box of tissue, and Rachel starts sharing the romantic details of the kiss. The next scene shows the guys gathered around a pizza. Joey asks about the kiss by saying, "Tongue?" Ross replies, "Yep," and that was the end of it. It was intended to show the humorous difference between men and women when talking about relationships, and though it was very funny, it was inaccurate.

Yes, some women do need to share all the details and talk to every girlfriend they know. But some men need to talk too. They don't always do it, though, because society tells them that's a girly thing to do. Again, it's more of a social-style issue, not a gender issue.

> No man ever looks at the world with pristine
> eyes. He sees it edited by a definite set of customs
> and institutions and ways of thinking.
> —Ruth Benedict

It's More About Social Style

So now you know that the amount a person talks is not based on gender—it's based on social style. Or more precisely, the amount a person *wants* to talk is not based on gender—it's based on social style. (See figures 1A and 1B to see the relationship between social styles and communication.) Certain social and cultural situations may lend themselves to men or women talking more. For example, who do you think talks more in Afghanistan—men or women? My guess would be men. Social acceptability and culture will play a role in how much someone may actually talk in a given situation, but social style will dictate how much they *want* to talk. If you take a little time to understand social style and how it affects behavior, you can begin to make adjustments to improve the personal and professional relationships in your life.

Analytical	Driver
Ask/Task	*Tell/Task*
Low desire to talk	High desire to talk
Amiable	**Expressive**
Ask/Relationship	*Tell/Relationship*
Low desire to talk	High desire to talk

Fig. 1A. Social styles and the desire to talk.

Analytical	Driver
Ask/Task	*Tell/Task*
Softer tone	Higher tone
Slower speed	Faster speed
Amiable	**Expressive**
Ask/Relationship	*Tell/Relationship*
Softer tone	Higher tone
Slower speed	Faster speed

Fig. 1B. Social styles, tone of voice, and speed of talk.

For Your Improvement

Reflect on the following questions and write down your answers. Save your answers and refer to them as you work toward the improvement of your personal and professional relationships.

1. What is your social style?

2. What have you learned from this chapter, and how could you effectively apply this information to your personal and professional life?

2

Men Are Slobs,
Women Are Neat

Marcus rushed home from the airport, hoping to get the computer room organized. This was his quiet place of refuge after a long day, and he considered it his home office. Normally, he knew exactly where everything was, and everything had its own place. His business journals were stacked on the upper right corner of the desk. The stapler and tape dispenser were neatly aligned just below the journals. A small, framed picture of his family was positioned on the upper left corner of the desk. The top drawer of his desk contained all of his home finance files, including previous tax returns and financial statements. The bottom drawer was filled with clearly marked files that ranged from "Current Projects" to "College Cost Comparisons for Children" to "Consumer Reports." Normally, when Marcus walked into the computer room, everything was exactly as he left it. But this day was different.

Marcus had been out of town for five days, and his sister had come to visit his wife, Carmen, while he was away. His sister had two teenage daughters who loved to spend hours on MySpace, and Marcus knew they probably ransacked his computer room. Carmen didn't seem to understand his need to have everything perfectly arranged, and she let her nieces hang out in the computer room while he was away.

When Marcus walked through the front door, he immediately tripped over a backpack. Trying to hide his frustration, he picked up the backpack, set it on a chair, and proceeded to give his wife a hug.

"How was your trip?" Carmen was excited to have him home.

"It was the same as always."

"Did you get to show them your new ideas for the software updates?"

"Yeah. They liked them." Marcus smiled but seemed a little distracted.

God made rainy days so gardeners
could get the housework done.
—anonymous

"That's great, honey. Listen, your sister went to the mall with the girls to do some school shopping. Do you want to have some coffee and catch up on what's been going on?"

"Actually, can we do that later? I would really like to get some things organized in the office and get a couple of things off my plate so I can relax." Carmen forced a smile and nodded understandingly as Marcus turned toward the computer room.

His steps slowed as he neared the door. His heart started to beat a little faster as he feared what might be behind that door. His hand reached for the doorknob as he drew in a long breath. He held his breath in anticipation as his hand turned the knob and inched the door open. He could no longer stand the suspense, so he thrust the door completely open. The music from *Psycho* rang in his head as his eyes darted around the room. His worst nightmare was unfolding. The stapler was on the floor. His journals were scattered across the desk. Pens were out of their container. Yellow sticky notes with drawings and smiley faces were plastered to his computer screen. He could feel the veins protruding in his neck!

As Marcus began to put everything back in its place, Carmen entered the room.

"Is everything all right, honey?"

"Yeah it's fine, Carmen. I just need to get some things done."

"Okay. Is there anything I can do to help?"

"Nope." Marcus didn't even look up as he continued to reorganize his office.

Carmen left the room thinking, *Typical male. Comes home, goes into his cave, and doesn't even want to talk.*

Unraveling the Scenario

As we look at this real-life scenario, we begin to see how some unhelpful gender stereotypes were perpetuated while others didn't fit. For example, this situation would appear to confirm that women talk more than men, women want relationships and men want to accomplish tasks, women pursue and men withdraw, or women want to talk at the end of the day and men want to retreat to their caves.

A deeper look into social style better explains the actions that are taking place. Additionally, once we examine and evaluate Marcus's and Carmen's social styles, we can start to understand why they are behaving the way they are. As we do this, we see that gender is not the driving issue—social style is.

I conducted a social style evaluation on Carmen and Marcus to confirm their respective social styles. I had a pretty good idea of what their social styles were by listening to their scenarios and observing their behavior, but the confirmation helped them understand why they do the things they do.

The evaluations revealed that Marcus is an Analytical and Carmen is an Expressive. They are complete opposites (see chart 2A).

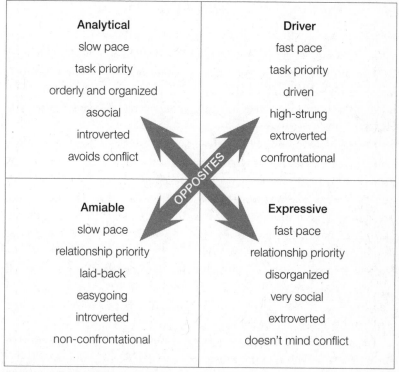

Analytical	**Driver**
slow pace	fast pace
task priority	task priority
orderly and organized	driven
asocial	high-strung
introverted	extroverted
avoids conflict	confrontational
Amiable	**Expressive**
slow pace	fast pace
relationship priority	relationship priority
laid-back	disorganized
easygoing	very social
introverted	extroverted
non-confrontational	doesn't mind conflict

OPPOSITES

Fig. 2A. Opposites in social style.

When we look at their situation with their social styles in mind, everything starts to make sense. Analyticals are very organized people. They don't like their stuff moved, and they don't like chaos. The Analytical knows exactly where to find everything, and he wants it left there. Analyticals are by nature task oriented, which means they gravitate toward getting tasks completed before socializing. In fact, Analyticals would prefer to stay clear of intensely social situations because they feel uncomfortable and awkward in those environments. Analyticals also avoid conflict and prefer to just keep things inside because they are introverted and think some things are better left unsaid.

Those proud of keeping an orderly desk
never know the thrill of finding something
they thought they had irretrievably lost.

—Helen Exley

Marcus is a very strong Analytical. He told me he actually felt immense stress when things were disorganized. He felt frustration when Carmen left things lying around, let the kids leave things strewn throughout the house (like the backpack at the door), and tolerated a constant state of chaos.

Carmen saw things a little differently. She said their home wasn't in a state of chaos at all. It just wasn't important to her to have everything in its perfect place. She hated routines and schedules and wanted lots of spontaneity. She said she was frustrated with Marcus and his need for routine, predictability, and constant order. She wanted to have more fun, talk more, and socialize with their friends more.

Carmen is a typical Expressive. Her desire to be more social has nothing to do with the fact that she's a woman. She simply has an Expressive social style. Her disorganization defies the gender myth that men are slobs and women are neat. Maybe some would argue that she is an anomaly. I would respectfully disagree.

Expressives who do not have a strong element of Driver or Analytical to them tend to be disorganized. (See appendix B: "Secondary Social Styles" and appendix C: "You're Some of All Four.") Their priority is to save energy for much more fun things than keeping everything in its exact place.

Why Women Are Complaining About Slobs

Men across the world have taken a bad rap for being slobs. Sitcoms perpetuate this stereotype, as do many movies. One of the main reasons you hear women complaining about men being slobs is that more women in the world live under the cultural gender *role*, or social norm, of keeping things clean. This is shifting as more and more wives work full-time outside the home.

Helene Couprie, a labor economist with the Universe of Toulouse, conducted a study on time allocation within the family that included how many hours men and women spend on household chores. In a study of more than 2000 people, here is what she found:

Single women spend an average of ten hours a week on housework.

Single men spend an average of seven hours a week on housework.

Women living with a man spend an average of fifteen hours a week on housework.

Men living with a woman spend an average of five hours a week on housework.

So why do men do less household work than women when single and even less when married? One might conclude that men are slobs and women are neat. Helene Couprie asserts that social norms are the reason. Men grow up watching women do all of the household chores, and guys are not taught how to keep a house clean. As a result, when they are single, they do less cleaning than single women who were raised with the social norms of women cleaning. Once a woman is living in the house with a man, he does even less housecleaning because he assumes she will do it. She now has to clean for two people, not just one, so her housework time increases.

My second-favorite household chore is
ironing. My favorite chore is hitting my
head on the top bunk bed until I faint.

—Erma Bombeck

In a different study conducted by the University of Maryland, the same type of trend emerged. The amount of time women spend on housework is down 40 percent over the past 38 years. This study showed men spending four and a half hours a week on household chores in 1965 compared to nine and a half hours a week by the year 2003. On a side note, a surprising result of the survey showed the amount of time mothers spend with their children actually went up from ten hours a week in 1965 to fourteen hours a week in 2003. ("Time spent with children" was defined as reading to them, playing games with them, feeding them, bathing them, and the like.)

I am very proud to be called a pig. It
stands for pride, integrity, and guts.
—Ronald Reagan

So as women entered the workforce in droves, the time spent on house-cleaning dropped for women and increased for men. The man and the woman in a household may both work full-time, but women still clean more. Again, this is not because women are neat and men are slobs; it's because social norms place most of the burden of cleaning on women. Social norms give other responsibilities to men, such as mowing the lawn, maintaining the car, cleaning the garage, and doing home repairs.

I have known plenty of women who are horrible cooks and men who are great in the kitchen. Conversely, I know plenty of women who are handy with tools and some men who don't know the difference between a wrench and a screwdriver. These things are determined largely by your experience growing up and what you were taught.

We had some friends over for a barbeque a number of years ago. One of the men decided to tell his favorite joke. He asked, "How many men does it take to clean a toilet?"

Someone humored him and said, "I don't know. How many?"

"None," he replied. "It's a woman's job."

I think he's still single today.

Who Works More, Men or Women?

Let's look at another myth. According to social norms, women care for the children and continue to do most of the household chores. Many of these women also work outside the home, so many people assume that women now work more than men do.

This is a pervasive assumption and has even been the topic of some popular talk show television programs. In a survey where the respondents were asked who they thought worked more, women or men, 70 percent of sociologists, 54 percent of economists, and 62 percent of economics students all said they thought women worked more. This survey was conducted by three economists (Michael Burda, Daniel Hamermesh, and Philippe Weil) who also examined the data from surveys from 25 countries.

The results of this 2007 study might surprise some people. In the United States, men spend an average of 2.7 hours each day on work in the home and 5.2 hours a day on work outside the home, totaling 7.9 hours a day. Women spend an average of 4.5 hours a day on work inside the home and 3.4 hours a day on work outside the home, totaling 7.9 hours. Interesting—the totals are exactly the same. (The averages included weekends, which brought the overall daily hours down.)

The myth: Women do more household chores than men and also work outside the home, so women must work more than men.

The truth: A 2007 study revealed that men and women work about the same amount of hours.

So this widely spread myth is apparently inaccurate. Social norms are changing the dynamics of household chores, so some of our gender stereotypes will probably change in the future. As men are given responsibility and credit for more of the housework, the idea that men are slobs and women are neat may change.

One Size Does Not Fit All

You will see Josh and Bri pop up in quite a few examples. One of the reasons is that they have distinct social styles. Also, they defy many of the gender stereotypes and would appear to confirm other stereotypes if you didn't understand social style. Besides, I have frequent interaction with them, so I am able to observe their behavior on an ongoing basis.

The stereotype of men being slobs and women being neat seems to fit

Josh and Bri. She keeps the house very clean. When it's not clean, she feels stressed. When Josh doesn't pick up after himself, she feels frustrated. Josh can't seem to understand why Bri needs to have the dinner dishes cleaned and put away before everyone has even left the table. He offers to do the dishes later, but to Bri, that just means she has to look at them stacked in the sink, and that stresses her out. She wants them done right away.

My theory on housework is, if the item doesn't multiply, smell, catch on fire, or block the refrigerator door, let it be. No one cares. Why should *you?*

—Erma Bombeck

Josh leaves his towel on the bathroom floor; Bri hangs hers on the hook. Josh leaves clothes lying around the bedroom; Bri puts them in their respective places. Josh leaves his hair gel and shaving cream sitting out on the counter; Bri prefers to have the bathroom counter clean. Josh leaves his mail sitting on the kitchen table; Bri bought him a mail basket, but he doesn't like it—he needs to see the mail to remind him that it needs to be processed. They adore each other, but they can't always understand why they are so different.

An outsider might say, "Well, Josh is a guy, men are slobs, and women are neat, so just deal with it." But that's not the whole story. Josh is an Expressive, and perfect organization is not a priority for him. Bri is an Analytical, and she can be obsessive about having things clean and organized. So the problem is not with gender but with social style. Fortunately, even though social style is innate and ingrained, we are free and responsible to choose our behaviors.

Dusting is a good example of the futility of trying to put things right. As soon as you dust, the fact of your next dusting has already been established.

—George Carlin

So even though having things clean isn't as high a priority for Josh as it is for Bri, he still makes an effort to go beyond his comfort zone and put things away or do the dishes sooner. And even though Bri's natural reaction is to want to have everything clean and perfect immediately, she still makes an effort to socialize and have fun with Josh when she can hear the dishes calling her name.

Understanding social style helps you identify innate differences and make behavior changes to accommodate each other. If you continue to attribute stereotypical gender myths to the opposite sex, you may find yourself trying to make accommodations that don't apply.

Survey Says

In my survey, I didn't ask people how many hours a week they spend on household chores. Instead, I asked respondents to mark the following statement true or false: "I keep things very neat, clean, and organized."

More men than women said they were neat, clean, and organized. In all fairness, more men than women responded to the survey (219 males versus 203 females). One sector that I sent an e-mail announcement to regarding the online survey was the fire service. There are predominately more males than females in the fire service.

Most of the respondents who said they were neat, clean, and organized were either Analyticals or Drivers. The vast majority of those who said they were not neat, clean, and organized were either Expressives or Amiables. Some of the secondary social styles played into the responses, but gender did not appear to determine whether people were neat or slobs.

It's More About Social Style

Being neat, clean, and organized has nothing to do with gender and everything to do with social style. It may appear to be gender related because of socially constructed gender *roles*, but the actual innate tendency to be organized is based on the social style you were born with.

Analyticals are normally very clean and organized people. Drivers also tend to have things neat and are sometimes even militant about being organized. Amiables are not as concerned with having everything perfect and tend to be accused of being too lazy and apathetic. If an Amiable thinks a messy house or work area may cause too much conflict with others, she will keep it clean to please other people. Expressives just don't care. "The clothes on the floor aren't hurting anybody, and I will eventually figure out where I put those files on my desk." Take a look at figure 2B for the tendencies of each social style.

Analytical	Driver
task oriented	task oriented
slow-paced	fast-paced
organized	organized
Amiable	**Expressive**
relationship oriented	relationship oriented
slow-paced	fast-paced
disorganized	disorganized

Fig. 2B. Social styles and organization.

So if you're a guy who has been throwing his clothes on the floor, you don't get to use the excuse that men are just slobs. And whether you're male or female, you don't get to use the excuse that you were just born that way as an Expressive or an Amiable. Show some consideration by adapting to the needs of the people you live with. Try to understand the stress Drivers and Analyticals feel when you leave things in disarray.

If you are an Analytical or a Driver, try to curb your obsessive-compulsive need to have things in perfect order. Drivers need to relax on the control issue, and Analyticals need to relax on the perfectionism issue. Lighten up a little and make accommodations for the Amiables and Expressives around you.

As you can see, creating more cohesive relationships requires plenty of compromise. Everyone needs to adapt to the social styles of the people they live and work with if they hope to improve their relationships.

For Your Improvement

Reflect on the following questions and write down your answers. Refer back to them as you work toward the improvement of your personal and professional relationships.

1. Does your personal social style lean more toward tidiness or messiness?

2. What can you do to be less irritating in this area for the people you live and work with?

3. Considering the social styles of the people you live and work with, how can you best adapt to them in this area?

4. What else have you learned from this chapter, and how could you effectively apply this information to your personal and professional life?

3

Men Are Leaders, Women Are Followers

This gender stereotype has been widely held throughout our society, and we shouldn't be surprised. Men have traditionally held most of the leadership roles all the way up to the president of the United States. It has been a cultural norm for men to take leadership roles in many circumstances. As a result, an assumption has emerged that men are natural leaders and women were born to be followers.

Some "experts" have built on this myth by claiming that…

- Women are not as ambitious as men.

- Women are not risk takers, so they don't make good leaders.

- Women tend to avoid confrontation and keep the peace because of their hormones. (All of the men reading this are laughing and thinking, *Wow! You have obviously never met my woman!*")

- Women are not as motivated as men.

- Women go against their own feminine nature when they try to lead.

- Women are too introverted to lead.

If your actions inspire others to dream more, learn more, do more, and become more, you are a leader.
—John Quincy Adams

Many of the alleged evidences of certain stereotypes actually contradict each other. For example, one stereotype asserts that women are too intro-verted, acquiescing, and apathetic to be leaders. They just aren't as assertive as men. Yet according to another gender stereotype, women are assertive in conflict, and men retreat to their caves. And we wonder why people are confused about gender issues!

Look at the bulleted list above. Each item is attributable to social style, not gender. Let's take a look at each one.

Ambition. Drivers and Expressives are naturally ambitious. Analyticals and Amiables tend to value stability and security.

Risk taking. This aspect of leadership follows ambition. Most people who are ambitious are willing to take risks. The risk-taking social styles are the Drivers and Expressives. Analyticals and Amiables tend to gravitate toward safety, not risk.

Confrontation. This gender myth about women has to be the biggest joke of them all. The idea that women can't excel in leadership positions because they don't like to deal with conflict is laughable. Yes, some women hate conflict (as do plenty of men), but this is not a gender issue—it's a social-style issue.

The only test of leadership is that somebody follows.

—Robert Greenleaf

Amiables and Analyticals avoid conflict. It makes them feel uncomfortable, and they would rather not deal with it. Amiables will give in to keep the peace, and Analyticals will withdraw to save face. You can easily see this tendency in both men and women who fall into these social style categories.

Drivers and Expressives do not mind confrontation. In fact, sometimes they look for it. They are assertive and opinionated, and they do not have a problem telling people what they think.

Motivation. People with differing social styles are motivated by differ-ent things and in different degrees. Drivers and Expressives are motivated to get things done quickly and may even make occasional rash decisions. Analyticals and Amiables are more methodical and tend to take longer to get things done. Drivers are often highly motivated, they are usually the most productive of the four social styles, and they are the most likely to become workaholics.

Nature. The idea that women who lead are at odds with their own feminine nature is absurd. If a woman is born a Driver or an Expressive, she will naturally lead in many situations. She may have reasons not to take on a leadership role, but that doesn't mean she doesn't desire to lead.

Introversion. People who are highly introverted and asocial do not generally excel in leadership roles. Therefore, people who believe that women are more introverted than men often believe that women are less likely to be effective leaders. But those who embrace the idea that women are introverted evidently haven't considered the countless Expressive and Driver women in the world.

Assertiveness, extroversion, and introversion are all attributable to social style, not gender. Plenty of introverted men do not do as well in social situations or certain leadership roles as social and extroverted women. Drivers and Expressives are the extroverts, and Amiables and Analyticals are the introverts. It's not about gender, it's about social style.

So does this mean Analyticals and Amiables can't be great leaders? Not at all. Many of the qualities of great leaders can be attributable to behaviors. Even with the natural traits you inherited with your social style, you are still free to choose your behavior. All four social styles can excel as leaders, and each style brings different traits to the table.

Breaking the Glass Ceiling

A 1987 book, *Breaking the Glass Ceiling: Can Women Reach the Top of America's Largest Corporations?* revealed the results of a three-year study on female executives in 25 different companies from various industries. It identified significant characteristics that more than 60 percent of these successful leaders shared, including these:

ability to manage subordinates

track record of achievement

willingness to take career risks

ability to be tough, decisive, and demanding

These traits are usually attributed to male leaders. Once you strip away the stereotypes, you can see that female leaders possess some of these same traits. If you look even closer, you will see that female leaders and male leaders who have the same social style also possess some of the same leadership traits and behaviors.

Studies on Women and Leadership

Some studies have allegedly shown that female leaders tend to collaborate, and male leaders tend be more assertive; women are more empathetic, and men are more autocratic; women socialize, and men systemize; men excel under stress (fight), and women cave under pressure (flight). But I would be interested in analyzing the data according to social style. I would bet money that the responses would show that the traits had more to do with social style than with gender.

We have done almost everything in pairs since Noah,
except govern. And the world has suffered for it.

—Bella Abzug

Another study compared male leaders with females in administrative positions. The study found that the men were assertive and ambitious, and the women were more passive and uninterested in promotion. Again, I would like to see the individuals in the two groups categorized by social style. The traits that were attributed to the men or to the women are likely to be based on their social style, not their gender.

I conducted a similar informal study on a much smaller scale. I found an organization that had six women in top leadership positions. I interviewed the women as well as some of their subordinates. The subordinates (both male and female) used these words to describe four of the women:

ambitious	motivator	decisive
assertive	intense	
visionary	blunt	

One leader was also described as ruthless. The subordinates described a fifth female leader with these words:

thoughtful	nonconfrontational	precise
organized	indecisive	sarcastic
perfectionist	serious	

The subordinates described the sixth leader this way:

friendly	empathetic	conflict avoider
collaborative	peacemaker	easygoing

Not all of these descriptions matched up to the gender stereotypes of females. Only the fifth and sixth leaders resembled the stereotype of a woman's leadership style. The first four leaders exhibited traits normally attributable to a man's leadership style. Of course, some experts would dismiss this as a role reversal. In other words, four of the six women are taking on these traits and behaviors because they have to in order to survive in a man's leadership world. The fifth and sixth were just being themselves.

Before determining the social style of each leader, I wrote down what I suspected each one would be. After thoroughly interviewing the subordinates on some of the behavior patterns of each leader, I had a pretty good idea of their respective social styles. I assumed that the first four leaders were either Drivers or Expressives, the fifth leader was an Analytical, and the sixth was an Amiable.

After meeting with the leaders individually and conducting a social style analysis on each one, my assumptions proved to be correct. Three of the first four females were Expressives, and one was a Driver. (She was the one accused of being ruthless.) The fifth leader turned out to be an Analytical with a secondary social style of Driver (which explains the sarcasm). The sixth leader emerged as an Amiable.

Blessed is the leader who seeks the
best for those he serves.
—anonymous

The leadership traits and behaviors these leaders exhibited had nothing to do with gender or the positions they held. They had everything to do with social style. This doesn't mean that people who end up in positions of power don't adapt their social styles, because they do. For example, Amiables who hate conflict may very well step up to discipline employees, but they hate the process, and they hate having to deal with it. A Driver wouldn't think twice about it.

So yes, we must learn to adapt our behavior as needed, but when you get down to what comes naturally to us, you will see that our social styles dictate our natural tendencies in leadership more than our gender does.

Plenty of studies dispute the idea that men are natural leaders and women are natural followers. Some studies have shown that men and women respond the same way to stress if the circumstances are the same. Other studies have shown women excelling in systemizing. Still other studies have proven that women are just as capable of strong leadership skills and abilities as men.

Comparisons based on gender can always be somewhat substantiated because some women are more empathizing (Amiables) and some men are more autocratic (Drivers). But of course, some women are more systemizing (Analyticals) and some men are more social (Expressives). So the debate can continue forever, or we can start to focus on social style and call a cease-fire from the war of the genders.

Survey Says

In my gender survey, I asked people if they tend to lead or follow. More men than women said they tend to lead. If we left it there, we could just reaffirm that men are natural leaders and women are natural followers. But once again, we need to dig deeper into the social style of the respondents. As I mentioned earlier, more Drivers and Expressives filled out the survey than Amiables or Analyticals. Additionally, I heard back from more male Drivers and Expressives than female.

The vast majority of people who said they tend to lead were Drivers and Expressives, regardless of gender. The majority of those who said they tend to follow turned out to be Amiables or Analyticals. You will find all four social styles in leadership positions, but Drivers and Expressives naturally tend to want to take the lead while Analyticals and Amiables don't mind surrendering the lead to others.

Most of the respondents who fell outside the norm had a secondary social style of Driver or Expressive. For example, when Analyticals answered that they tend to lead, their secondary social styles were usually either Driver or Expressive, not Amiable.

Breaking the Mold

Many couples feel as if they don't fit the mold. If they go to counseling, they may be told that they are experiencing a role reversal. If they read books on relationships, they might be told the shift in culture and gender roles is playing a part in the way they are responding to each other. Few experts are explaining that social style is the main contributor to the behaviors they are experiencing.

Chuck and Tracey agreed to fill out the gender survey. Tracey sent me an e-mail after completing the survey to give me some insight on how they are often viewed.

> My husband and I don't fit many of the typical stereotypes. I am the leader; he is the follower. I am practical; my husband is romantic—he loves to cuddle (I just want to go to sleep). I am much more independent, and I talk a lot more than he does! We have been married for twenty years, and this works for us. It might sound as though I am putting him down, but I love him the way he is. He just can't handle the stress of worrying about finances or paying the bills. I have always done it, and it doesn't bother me. He has no idea when the kids' doctor appointments are, or his own for that matter. I keep track of everything. It sure sounds like I'm tooting my own horn, but my husband does more things for me than I can tell you. He is taxi to the kids and takes them everywhere. Last week when my sweet little dog died, my husband was up all hours burying her for me because I couldn't. When I'm not feeling well, he doesn't leave my side. Please tell me what man would be fine with having his mother-in-law move in permanently? That's my husband, a wonderful guy. He's kind, sensitive, caring, and romantic.

As we dissect Tracey's e-mail, we see many areas where she and Chuck do not fit the gender stereotypes, including leadership, romance, nurturing, independence, and reaction to stress. Yet Tracey says she talks the most, so that would fit the stereotype that women talk more than men.

If we examine Tracey's and Chuck's social styles, her description of their relationship starts to make sense. Tracey's primary social style emerged as Expressive, and her secondary style is Driver (split very close to the middle, meaning she shows lots of traits of both styles). Chuck's primary social style is Amiable, and his secondary style is Expressive.

Tracey naturally gravitates toward taking the lead because as an Expressive and a Driver, she wants things done now. The Driver side of her is independent and practical. She can handle large amounts of stress and doesn't mind taking on a lot of responsibility.

We still think of a powerful man as a born leader
and a powerful woman as an anomaly.

—Margaret Atwood

Chuck's Amiable and Expressive combination makes for a very relationship-oriented person. He is not the stereotypical male. He is romantic and sensitive to other people's feelings. He is accommodating and doesn't care for conflict. He would prefer to avoid high levels of stress and appreciates that his wife takes on the things that stress him out.

I have countless other stories and interviews just like Chuck and Tracey's. Plenty of women are natural leaders. That doesn't mean they become CEOs of every organization they work in. Some aren't even in the workforce. Some are business owners, some are stay-at-home moms, some are single, and some are married. Regardless of their situations, these women have a natural tendency to take the lead with their friends, at work, in conversations, and with their significant others. They may relinquish leadership roles in certain situations for various reasons, but that doesn't stop their innate desire to take the bull by the horns. They are just made that way.

When you start to examine behavior through the paradigm of social style, you begin to see trends in specific behavior. Because of the stereotypes that exist, men often feel put down or less macho if they are not pushing themselves into leadership roles or taking inordinate amount of risks in their lives. Women often feel judged or put down if they take the lead and make things happen. "It's not ladylike." Assertiveness and the desire to lead comes from social style, not gender. Additionally, your style as a leader (whether passive or assertive, strict or lenient) also comes from social style, not gender. Let's take a look at the four social styles from the perspective of leadership.

The Analytical as a Leader

Analytical leaders are often professional and self-disciplined. They can make decisions logically and carefully. They excel in establishing policies, schedules, routines, and procedures. They can handle large amounts of details simultaneously regardless of whether they are male or female.

Followers often complain that the systematic thoroughness of the Analytical can turn into picky perfectionism (being nitpicky is an issue for Analytical men and women). This trait of the Analytical also shows up in the decision-making process—the Analytical would rather make no decision than a bad decision.

Analyticals are great at preserving the traditions of an organization but can be resistant to change. They are orderly and organized leaders.

The Driver as a Leader

Drivers are the most productive leaders you could hope to meet. They excel in making decisions and getting things done. Drivers would rather make a bad decision than no decision. They are visionaries who inspire people to overcome obstacles and achieve goals.

Drivers are great change agents but can become human tornados when things are not going as they would like them to. They can be bossy, stubborn, and demanding (regardless of whether they are male or female).

Drivers are great at starting big, complicated projects, but they don't like to maintain them. They will pass the maintenance on to someone else. They live and breathe the big picture but chafe under details.

Drivers can be cold and unfeeling leaders. They can be tough, sarcastic, and impatient. Drivers despise laziness and frivolity on the job. They have very little patience for perceived incompetence. Drivers expect others to be productive and work at very high levels as they do.

The Amiable as a Leader

Amiables don't always like to be in leadership roles, but when they are, they excel in getting along with others and making them feel comfortable. They are friendly and cooperative in their contact with employees, administrative staff, vendors, and just about everyone else they come into contact with. Amiables are usually ready to help others and be team players. Followers appreciate these leaders' supportive, easygoing nature.

> Being in power is a lot like being a lady. If you
> have to tell people you are, you aren't.
> —Margaret Thatcher

They shy away from conflict and will often avoid disciplining subordinates. Amiable leaders especially have a difficult time terminating employees, even when the employees become burdens to the organizations. Amiables will put off dealing with conflict as long as possible and may delay decisions that could offend others.

Amiables are great mediators as leaders. They excel in bringing people together and trying to help people get along. They are diplomatic and will go to great extremes to keep the peace.

The Expressive as a Leader

Expressive leaders like to have fun and create excitement in the organization. They are usually upbeat, and most people enjoy being around them. They are optimistic and playful leaders.

Expressives are also spontaneous, talkative, and personable. They have the persuasive power to stimulate action and get people to join in. They could sell ice cubes to Eskimos. Their charisma and charm make them great at selling their ideas and their vision.

Expressive leaders can also be loud, obnoxious, and downright insulting. If they are displeased with something, everyone within earshot will know about it. They can also be highly emotional, impulsive, and excitable.

They sometimes show up late for meetings and forget important appointments. They hate routine, rules, and boredom. Expressives want to have fun at their jobs, and they usually bring fun into the work environment with them.

It's More About Social Style

As you can see, leadership is not about gender, it's about social style. People with any of the four styles can be leaders, and they each have unique strengths and weaknesses. Some of the traits that have been attributed to women appear in the different social styles and can show up in males as well. Conversely, some of the traits that have been attributed to men can be found in the different social styles in both men and women. So as you can see, your style of leadership is not dictated by your gender—it's dictated by your social style. And even then, you can choose behavior that does not come naturally to you. It just takes a little practice...or maybe a *lot* of practice. See figure 3A for a summary of the social style leadership attributes.

Analytical	Driver
task oriented	task oriented
systematic	autocratic
perfectionist	productive
nonconfrontational	confrontational
detail oriented	visionary
content	ambitious
independent	independent
not a risk taker	risk taker
introvert	extrovert
strict on rules	strict on rules
Amiable	**Expressive**
relationship oriented	relationship oriented
nonconfrontational	confrontational
collaborator	motivator
detail oriented	visionary
complacent	ambitious
dependent	dependent
not a risk taker	risk taker
introvert	extrovert
lenient on rules	lenient on rules

Fig. 3A. Social style and leadership attributes.

The Leadership Power Struggle

The gender wars in leadership circles could be easily solved with one very effective leadership model: servant leadership. In fact, most of the power struggles that exist in leadership regardless of gender could be solved with this model. Servant leadership begins with a desire to serve others and be a role model of the behavior you expect. If you want others to treat you with courtesy and respect, set the example.

The first step to leadership is servanthood.

—John Maxwell

The concept of servant leadership was formalized in a book by Robert Greenleaf in 1977 called *Servant Leadership: A Journey into the Nature of Legitimate Power and Greatness.* However, the concept of being a servant to others, even as a leader, dates back thousands of years. The best role model of servant leadership is the most well-known and widely followed leader in history, the only leader who ever split time in half: Jesus Christ. He washed the feet of His followers to demonstrate what leadership really looked like. He didn't demand His own way, and His entire leadership philosophy centered on doing what was best for others, not Himself.

When you think of leadership in terms of serving others, you can set aside power struggles and seek to improve the lives of those around you. When you do, your own life will be improved in the process.

For Your Improvement

Reflect on the following questions and write down your answers. Refer back to them as you work toward the improvement of your personal and professional relationships.

1. Do you usually prefer to take the lead or let someone else lead?

2. How does this relate to your social style?

3. How can you use the natural tendencies of your social style to improve as a leader and a follower? What natural tendencies do you need to be careful of?

4. What else have you learned from this chapter, and how could you effectively apply this information to your personal and professional life?

4

Women Are Listeners, Men Tune You Out

M elissa was beginning to wonder if Ted was actually paying attention. She was so excited about her new promotion, and yet he seemed indifferent. She continued with her story.

"My boss said I was a great team player, and I was especially good at motivating people to get involved. He announced my promotion at a staff meeting, and I could see Janie turning green with envy. She has been sucking up for months trying to get that promotion. Everyone sees right through her. You met her at the company Christmas party three months ago, remember?"

Unfortunately, Ted had already checked out of the conversation and was running through the list of things he had to get done at the office the next day. He suddenly sensed the awkward silence and finally spoke. "That is so great, honey. I am really proud. You have worked so hard for this promotion, and you certainly deserve it."

"Have you even been listening to me?" Melissa was visibly annoyed.

"Of course I have."

"So what I did I just say?"

"You said you got a promotion. I heard you. I *am* listening!"

"That's not all I said! I was talking about Janie being jealous. You weren't even paying attention."

Ted was starting to get annoyed himself. "I got the gist of it. You were talking about your promotion, right? Why do you have to get hung up on the little details? Just cut to the chase and give me the bottom line."

"You know what? Just forget it. It's obviously not important enough to you for you to listen." Melissa stormed out of the room thinking, *What a typical guy! He never listens!*

Ted was left in the room thinking, *What a typical woman. Blah blah blah blah! Why can't she just get to the point?*

Frequent scenarios like this feed the gender stereotype that women are great listeners and men tune you out. In the real-life situation above, as it turns out, they both stink at listening. Melissa is an Expressive, and Ted is a Driver. Amiables and Analyticals appear to be better listeners because they don't talk as much or interrupt as much as Drivers and Expressives. Drivers and Expressives tend to interrupt, interject, or talk over the top of you. Even if they have learned to not do those things, they usually aren't listening—they're just waiting to talk.

When you are talking to Drivers like Ted, they might be thinking, *Does your train of thought have a caboose?* Drivers do not like to engage in long, drawn-out stories. Expressives are also impatient listeners because they want their turn. They love stories, but they prefer to be the narrators. Amiables listen well and don't want to be rude by interrupting or correcting people. They just want everyone to get along. Analyticals also listen well, but they would prefer not to be engaged in long conversations if they have tasks that need to be done.

Men have been raked over the coals on this stereotype. You see it in movies, commercials, and sitcoms. You hear about it in everyday conversations. Studies continue to emerge telling us why men have problems listening. Of course, they start with the premise that men don't listen.

When you are arguing with a fool, make
sure he isn't doing the same thing.
—anonymous

One study asserts that men listen primarily with the left side of the brain and women listen with both sides. It goes on to state that the right side of the brain attaches emotional meaning to words and that may be why women listen better (again, making the assumption that women actually *do* listen better) and why men tune out (making the assumption that all men tune women out). But this line of thinking has one very big problem: Not all men have a problem listening. Some experts would assert that these men are the exception, but the exceptions are far too common to ignore.

Men are often portrayed as insensitive jerks who don't listen to the needs of their sweet, tender, sensitive, emotional wives or girlfriends. Men just tune them out. Yes, some men don't listen well, but let's take a reality check: Some women don't listen too well either. This is much more of a social style and skill development issue than a gender issue.

Men Want to Solve Problems, Women Want to Be Heard

Let's look at another myth that is intertwined with the listening myth. The myth states that all men want to fix your problems when you talk to them, and women just want to be heard.

When you share something with Drivers or Expressives, their natural response is to give you advice, tell you what to do, and solve the problem. This is true whether the Driver or Expressive is a male or a female. How many times have you heard someone complain about a mother-in-law always giving unwanted advice or a female friend who won't just listen but insists on trying to solve the problem? It happens all the time. This isn't a gender issue, it's a social-style issue. Analyticals and Amiables are better about not pushing their thoughts and opinions on others. Drivers and Expressives need to work on it.

◀ ▶

The myth: Men want to fix everything and solve your problems when you talk to them, and women just want to be heard.

The truth: Drivers and Expressives tend to want to give you their advice and opinions. Analyticals and Amiables are better at just listening to you.

◀ ▶

Survey Says

In my survey, I asked people to respond to this true or false statement: "I am often accused of being a poor listener." More men than women said they were accused of being poor listeners. Once again, if we left the research at that, we could confirm that women are better listeners than men. Instead, we have to dig deeper into social style to discover the real truth.

Drivers and Expressives do not listen as well as Amiables and Analyticals. More Drivers and Expressives filled out the survey than Amiables or Analyticals. Additionally, of those Drivers and Expressives, men outnumbered women. The respondents who said they had difficulty listening were mostly

Drivers and Expressives. Here is an interesting piece of data that came out of the survey: The respondents who said they were not poor listeners but emerged as Drivers or Expressives were all over the age of 50. Interesting. Is it possible that as people mature and learn better skills, they can become better listeners even if it doesn't come naturally for them? I think so.

A Seasoned Listener

Norm was 88 years old when I sat down with him. He had kind eyes and a warm smile. He chose his words carefully, and when it was my turn to talk, he listened intently, leaned forward, and nodded his head. He asked questions and showed a high level of interest in what I was saying. He never interrupted me once and made me feel as if what I had to say was incredibly important. By all accounts this man was an outstanding listener. Surely he could not have been a Driver or an Expressive. But when I asked him a series of questions to determine his social style, I discovered he was indeed a Driver. What accounted for his great listening skills? According to Norm himself, a learned skill was the difference.

"You should have seen me as young man. I had the world by the tail—or so I thought. I knew it all, and I let everyone around me know that I knew it all. I could argue with the best of 'em. My wife would tell you I had the attention span of a gnat. Didn't listen to a word she said. It took years and years of learning the hard way how to be a good listener."

So I asked Norm if he thought people could change social styles. "Maybe you were a Driver when you were younger and now you're an Amiable." He held the same belief on this as I did.

"I'm still the same guy inside when it comes to my natural instinct. I still feel that urge to correct people or jump in while they are talking. I've just learned not to. The more you practice it, the easier it becomes. I've learned through the years that other people have a lot to teach me, but I can't learn much while I'm talking. I need to be listening. And listening isn't just waiting to talk—it's trying to understand what someone else is attempting to communicate."

People who know little, say much. People
who know much, say little.
—anonymous

What a wise man. Norm hit on my theory of social style. You are born with a distinct social style, and you will always have it. If you are born a Driver, you will die a Driver. But as you journey through life, you can choose to take on the positive traits of all four social styles to give yourself a better balance. You can choose behaviors that complement your strengths and cease behaviors that magnify your weaknesses. Your social style defines your natural tendencies, but it doesn't control your every behavior—your free choice does.

Good News, Bad News

I talked with Celia about her listening skills. Celia is a high-level executive with 15 subordinates. The organization Celia works for conducts 360-degree evaluations. This means a variety of people provide input and feedback about the effectiveness of the managers and employees. Celia's boss fills out an evaluation form, and so do her employees, coworkers, vendors, and clients. This is a positive and constructive way to get feedback, and Celia actually appreciates it. She confided in me that she consistently gets constructive criticism about her listening skills.

"I am always being told that I don't listen very well. It's hard to admit, but I guess I don't. I tend to get excited and interject when people are talking. Or if I think people are wrong, I don't let them finish before I correct them. I find myself finishing people's sentences if they are taking too long. It's hard to focus sometimes too. I find myself thinking about all of the things I need to get done, and I tend to tune people out, especially if they are too chatty. I get bored with conversations really easily and find myself wishing I were doing something else. What's wrong with me? Women are supposed to be great listeners."

I assured Celia that nothing was wrong with her and that the idea that women were great listeners was simply a misguided stereotype. I asked her a series of questions and discovered that Celia was a Driver, just like Norm. I explained to her what this meant and went over some of her natural tendencies. We talked about her busy mind and drive to get tasks done and her reluctance to simply chat with people. I explained that her social style was prone to tune out idle chatter and focus on tasks that need to be done. She was amazed at how on target this was with her tendencies.

After discussing how normal she was and assuring her that nothing was wrong with her, I broke the tough news. Her social style was no excuse for not improving her listening skills. Just because you have a natural tendency toward something doesn't mean you can't control it. That is the beauty of free choice and responsibility. When Celia became aware of her social style, she had an obligation to improve in an area that was affecting her relationships. We spent some time discussing some ways she could do just that. (See the section at the end of this chapter on how to improve your listening skills.)

What Does This Mean for You?

If you're an Expressive, your natural inclination is to dominate conversations instead of actively listening. When you are in conflict with people you are closest to, you might interrupt, interject, and overwhelm. If you want to improve any of your relationships, the first thing you need to do is listen! Let me give you an example of a typical Expressive in a conversation. We'll call him John.

> Steve: "Hey, John, how's it going?"
>
> John: "Great, bud—how are you?"
>
> Steve: "Couldn't be better. We just got back from Hawaii, and it was fantastic!"
>
> John: "I love Hawaii. We went last year and had a blast. We took a helicopter tour, and my wife about had a heart attack!"
>
> Steve: "Is that so?"
>
> John: "Yeah, it was insane! We came down this one hill, and I could swear we were going to hit the ground. The pilot was a maniac. It was quite the adrenaline rush. We're going back to Hawaii next year. My sister owns a condo there, so we can use it anytime we want."

The conversation would proceed with John sharing about John as long as Steve had the patience to listen (which would depend on Steve's social style). Expressives often take the ball and run with it, not even realizing they took over someone's story or conversation. Once you become aware of your tendency to do this, you will catch yourself and hopefully correct it. If you're an Expressive, learn to hold your tongue. Let people tell their story. Ask questions. Get involved with their interest. Then, when they are all done, you can share your story.

If you're in a personal or professional relationship with an Expressive, you need to know that Expressives love to talk, regardless of their gender. They like to talk about themselves and their interests, and they love to joke around a lot. They can get volatile and loud in conflict, but they do like to talk about their relational issues and work through them. If you're dealing with a male, don't simply assume he would rather go into his cave and not talk at all.

If you're a Driver, your natural inclination is to be right and to correct everyone. You probably don't mind debating issues. This annoys people. You may be an impatient listener, like the Expressive. When people are talking, you are likely to be thinking about what you want to say or the next point of your argument. Let your Amiable and Analytical counterparts talk more. More importantly, learn how to say, "I could be wrong." I know that's scary when you're thinking, *But what if I'm not wrong? I'm usually right!* Well, it's better to say you could be wrong and save face than to insist you are right and have your mistake shoved in your face. Besides, even if you are right, it bugs people that you rarely ever admit that you could be wrong.

If you're in a relationship with a Driver, you need to know that even though Drivers are usually extroverts, they tend to focus on tasks more than relationships. That means when they are working on a task, they would rather not be bothered with idle conversation. Get to your point and provide a Driver with the bottom line as quickly as possible so he or she can get back to work.

If you're an Amiable, you likely don't need to share your opinion, especially if you think it might offend others. So while you want to talk about your relationship issues and work them out, you tend to suck it up and let people walk all over you at times to save relationships. Try to speak your mind more and let people know how you really feel about things. Don't be afraid to tell Drivers or Expressives that they are talking too much and that you would like them to listen to your opinion.

> It takes two to speak the truth—one
> to speak and another to hear.
> —Henry David Thoreau

When you relate with Amiables, gently coax them to share their thoughts and opinions. They actually do want to talk about their relationship issues but not with someone who will dominate the conversation or overwhelm them with demonstrative behavior. Lower your voice and speak calmly with Amiables. Let them know they can safely share their feelings. Show courtesy, respect, and kindness as you listen, and they will usually open up to you.

If you're an Analytical, you also tend to avoid conflict by letting Drivers and Expressives dominate conversations. You might want to retreat into a cave and analyze things thoroughly before talking about them. By then, no one it is interested anymore. Try to understand that some people (Drivers and Expressives) want to address issues much quicker and solve them. So try to push yourself a little outside your comfort zone and openly talk about what is going on with you.

If you're in a relationship with an Analytical, try to understand that too many relationship issues will overwhelm Analyticals (this is true with Drivers as well). Approach Analyticals logically and methodically to deal with issues. If you are overly emotional, you will just drive them away, and they will tune you out (regardless of whether they are male or female). Analyticals, like Drivers, work logically, not emotionally (unlike Expressives and Amiables). Try to harness your emotions when having conversations with Analyticals, and you will get them to talk and open up more as well as actively listen.

> You cannot truly listen to anyone and do
> anything else at the same time.
> —M. Scott Peck

I mentioned early in this chapter that Amiables and Analyticals can often appear to be better listeners because they don't talk as much or interrupt as much as Drivers or Expressives. Well, just for the record, being silent while someone is talking does not necessarily mean you are listening. If you are clamming up to avoid conflict or thinking about other things while you act like you're listening, you still need to work on your active listening skill (see chapter 14). See figure 4A for a summary of social styles and communication.

Analytical	Driver
good listener	poor listener
avoids confrontation	debater
withdraws in conflict	opinionated
overanalyzes	hates to admit wrongs
reserved	stubborn
softer tone	blunt
Amiable	**Expressive**
good listener	poor listener
doesn't offer opinions	talks a lot
avoids conflict	tells lots of stories
quiet	loud
easily gives in	opinionated
agreeable	demonstrative

Fig. 4A. Social styles and communication.

For Your Improvement

Reflect on the following questions and write down your answers. Refer back to them as you work toward the improvement of your personal and professional relationships.

1. How would you rate your current listening skills—poor, fair, good, or excellent?

2. How does this relate to your social style?

3. What natural tendencies of your social style can you build on or improve to become a better listener and share your true thoughts more effectively?

4. What else have you learned from this chapter, and how could you effectively apply this information to your personal and professional life?

5

Women Are Romantic, Men Are Practical

Mushy. That's how many women are portrayed in love or romance. Every woman loves to get flowers. Every woman loves touchy-feely cards. Every woman aches to be taken out to a candlelight dinner and a sunset walk along a sandy beach. Every woman wants her man to have a hot bubble bath waiting for her when she comes home.

Men, on the other hand, are practical. They don't go for all that romance stuff and merely go through the motions because they know that's what women want and because all the romance will probably lead to more sex.

Surely you have met plenty of men and women who would beg to differ with these stereotypes. Many men consider themselves very romantic, and plenty of women think of themselves as more practical than romantic. Some people are more romantic than others because of their social style, not their gender.

I read an article recently about the way men and women view romance. College students were asked what their favorite romantic movies were. The number one answer for both men and women was *Sleepless in Seattle*. But their second choice differed: The men chose *The Princess Bride*, and the women chose *While You Were Sleeping*. The article went on to say that men and women viewed romance differently, but by their movie choices, they didn't seem too far apart in this particular example. One respondent commented that "Most girls dream of these romantic situations, the kind that end happily."

Do women honestly think that men dream about relationship situations that don't end happily? Men don't wake up thinking, *You know, I think I will get myself into a relationship situation that ends miserably. That sounds great!*

Romance has been elegantly defined as
the offspring of fiction and love.
—Benjamin Disraeli

Both men and women want cohesive relationships. However, the amount of romance or relational interaction they desire will vary according to their social style, not their gender. In fact, the data regarding gender is not consistent. Some experts insist that men are actually more romantic than women, perhaps because men are more visually oriented and allegedly fall in love faster. One study concludes that more men remarry and that men are more dependent on their girlfriends or wives because they have fewer close friends than women and less meaningful relationships with their other family members.

Another expert conducted a telephone survey of 1000 Americans, in which 56 percent of the men felt romantic on vacations while only 46 percent of the women did. If we considered only the gender issue in these studies, we might draw an inaccurate conclusion that men are more romantic than women.

In another interesting study, a Kansas State professor discovered that men actually like romantic movies more than they admit or more than people might assume they do. The stereotype that is placed on men often causes men to appear macho lest people may think they are sissies.

Another fun survey asked men what types of Valentine's Day cards they preferred to receive: sexy/naughty, comedic, or romantic. The stereotypes about men promoted in movies, sitcoms, and the media would lead you to believe that men would have overwhelming picked sexy/naughty, with comedic coming in close second and romantic scraping the bottom.

There are two sorts of romantics: those who love,
and those who love the adventure of loving.
—Lesley Blanch

Surprise! Only 10 percent of the men said they would want a sexy/naughty card. A third of the men said they would prefer a comedic card, and a third said they would prefer receiving a romantic card. I don't know what the remaining men said, but they were probably Analyticals who thought, *Don't get me a card at all—it's a waste of money.*

I would love to study the data in the light of social style and see if the gender distinctions are not as significant as most people think.

Survey Says

In my survey, I asked people to indicate whether they were more practical or more romantic. More women than men said they were more romantic than practical. Doesn't that confirm the stereotype? Well, it would if we left it at that. Once we examine the social style of the respondents, we see that the relationship-oriented people are more romantic, and the task-oriented people are more practical.

Expressives and Amiables tend to consider themselves more romantic than Drivers and Analyticals do. More male Expressives than female filled out the survey, but more female Amiables responded than male. Overall, more female relationship-oriented social styles filled out the survey than male relationship-oriented social styles.

The vast majority of Expressives and Amiables chose romance over practicality, regardless of their gender. The majority of Analyticals and Drivers chose practicality over romance—women as well as men.

Sometimes the Stereotypes Are Backward

I interviewed Martin and Jackie about their different feelings about romance. I waited until after the interview to analyze their social styles.

Martin did most of the talking in the interview. He was animated and passionate when he spoke. He joked a lot and reached over to take Jackie's hand on several occasions during the interview. She smiled and seemed to enjoy watching him tell the story.

"Jackie and I are so incredibly different when it comes to this issue. Some of our friends think we have reversed roles. I am Mr. Romantic and she is Mrs. Practical. When we were first dating and in the early years of our marriage, I would bring flowers home for Jackie. She was always kind and appreciative, but I could always tell she was hesitant to tell me what she really liked. She didn't want to hurt my feelings."

Jackie nodded her head in agreement. Martin continued. "After four years of marriage, she finally got up the nerve to tell me that she loved my thoughtfulness, but she thought flowers were a waste of money. They died quickly, and she didn't particularly care for the strong smell. She told me that she preferred we use the money for something more useful. I was shocked! I thought all women wanted flowers."

I asked Jackie what she thought Martin's preferences were when it came to romance. "Well, when we were first married I just thought he was a very attentive man who had read lots of books about how to romance a woman. He took me out to nice dinners, walks on the beach, and romantic vacations. But when I became more comfortable telling him what my preferences were, I realized that he did a lot of this stuff because *he* liked all the romance. I kept thinking we couldn't afford these vacations and we really should be putting the money into our retirement accounts instead. His argument was that our relationship was more important and that we needed to focus on that more."

The myth: Men aren't interested in romance. They are practical and engage in romance because they have to. Women live for romance and want frivolous gifts showered on them constantly.

The truth: Expressives and Amiables consider themselves more romantic than practical. Drivers and Analyticals consider themselves more practical than romantic.

Martin could barely sit still while she was talking. He couldn't wait to pipe in. "I started to think maybe she didn't feel the same way about me as I did her. I wanted to spend time around her in romantic settings and just talk. That didn't seem to be as important to her, and I couldn't figure out why."

I had to smile as I listened to both of them. If they only knew how normal they really were. After a lengthy discussion on their relationship, we proceeded to determine their social styles. I had a hunch that Martin was an Expressive and Jackie was an Analytical. I had each of them fill out a social style questionnaire. Sure enough, my hunch was correct.

I explained to this couple that Expressives prefer more romance than Analyticals do, and Analyticals are much more practical than Expressives. I also pointed out that Expressives tend to talk more and confront conflict head-on and that Analyticals talk less and tend to withdraw in conflict. I proceeded to explain some of the differences and tendencies in their social styles. By the look on their faces, you would think I had just read their minds. The light came on for both of them. Martin threw his hands in the air and shouted "Well, no wonder!" Jackie sat with a sly smile on her face, and I sensed her Analytical mind racing to put it all in its proper place.

"I always felt different from the stereotypical woman, and I never felt like I could fit into that mind-set. I always appreciated a good love story in a movie, but some of the over-the-top mushy stuff felt pretty sappy. I just thought, *Get real! This is like a fairy tale. Let's get back to reality!*"

Martin added his two cents. "Yeah, and my friends kept making fun of me, saying things like, 'You're such a skirt!' This really makes sense to me now."

In a great romance, each person basically
plays a part that the other really likes.
—anonymous

Martin and Jackie had struggled for years trying to make sense of each other. They had even purchased books on relationships, where Martin read that men need to be more romantic and Jackie was told that women need to have sex and then let their man retreat to his cave. It wasn't working for them, and it doesn't work for the millions of other couples who don't fit these molds.

When you strip away the gender stereotypes and look at social style tendencies, you get a much better idea of why you are the way you are and do the things you do. Some women aren't naturally romantic, and some men aren't naturally practical. Our culture tells men that being romantic or desiring romance is not macho, so many men will just stuff their desires. Women are surrounded by messages that say all women need romance, so many women are afraid to tell their husband that they would prefer he wash the car than bring her flowers. Learning the social style of the one you love will help you understand what he or she appreciates and values.

How to Show Love to Drivers

As we have seen, Drivers tend to be practical. In fact, they can be cynical about romance. If things get too emotional, they get uncomfortable. They are not touchy-feely and prefer you do practical things for them. They are task oriented, so getting stuff done is high on their list. If you want to show a Driver you care, do what you said you would do, when you said you would, the way you said you would. Follow through on your commitments and be dependable. Here is a list of ways to show Drivers you care:

> Be responsible, dependable, and punctual.
>
> Complete every project you start. Follow through on your commitments.
>
> Wash the car, mow the lawn, or organize the garage.
>
> Clean up after yourself. Do the dishes, clean the house, make the bed.
>
> Engage in challenging or competitive activities.
>
> Recognize and compliment their ability to set goals and reach them.
>
> Show admiration for their leadership abilities.
>
> Buy a gift.

How to Show Love to Expressives

Expressives love things that are fun, exotic, and romantic. They are adventurous and spontaneous. Being practical is often not a high priority for these folks. They want to enjoy life, love, and relationships, and if that means being frivolous, then so be it. Expressives love physical touch and contact, and that is a great way to show them romance. They also appreciate gifts and surprises. Being the center of attention is fun for them, so they love parties. Here are some ways to show love to Expressives:

> Be spontaneous and unpredictable. Surprise them.
>
> Touch them: kiss them hello and goodbye, hug, hold hands, and cuddle.
>
> Ask what type of physical touch is most important to them.
>
> Go on dates that are adventurous and fun.

Loosen up and have a sense of humor.

Buy fun and frivolous gifts.

Give them your time and attention. Throw them parties.

Compliment their fun and outgoing nature.

Show admiration for their ability to stay young at heart.

How to Show Love to Analyticals

Analyticals are very practical. They need to feel secure, and they are concerned about spending money wisely. Buying impractical gifts or being frivolous with Analyticals is not necessary. They are task-oriented (like Drivers) and appreciate you for getting things done. They also appreciate gifts that are practical (something they can really use). Here are some ideas for how you can show love to an Analytical:

Buy practical gifts.

Spend money wisely.

Keep your home clean and organized.

Ask them what areas of organization are most important to them.

Be trustworthy and predictable. Have procedures and follow them. Build traditions.

Show them softness and kindness.

Do things with a high level of quality.

Complete tasks for them.

Compliment their sacrifice, loyalty, and analytical ability.

How to Show Love to Amiables

Amiables prefer romance over practicality, but they are not as vocal about it as Expressives are. Amiables are relationship oriented, but they are shy and avoid conflict. As a result, they don't always tell their significant other what they would really like because they don't want to hurt the other person's feelings. They love kind words of appreciation and sincerity. Amiables want to spend quality time with the people they love. Here are some ways to show love to Amiables:

> Spend lots of one-on-one time together.
>
> Show compassion.
>
> Tell them that you love them, like them, accept them, and think about them often.
>
> Assure them that conflict will not end the relationship.
>
> Affirm your commitment to them.
>
> Ask them what assurances are most important to them.
>
> Take them on quiet, romantic dates.
>
> Show gentleness.
>
> Exercise patience.
>
> Buy them sentimental gifts.
>
> Give them sincere praise.
>
> Show appreciation for their kindness and giving nature.
>
> Show admiration for their ability to get along with people easily.

As you can see, not all women are cuddle bunnies, and not all men shirk affection. Romance comes wrapped in a very different package for each social style. Unfortunately, we tend to show others love and romance in the way we want people to show it to us. But if I am an Expressive social style who loves risk, excitement, and adventure, that may not go over well with an Amiable who prefers safety, calmness, and quiet. We need to do unto others as they would have us do unto them.

This requires learning the social style of those we care about. It's easy to do, and once you get the hang of it, you can identify social style simply by observing behavior. Be sure to look at appendix A to determine your own social style and the social style of your significant other. Because of secondary social styles, you may find that your Analytical spouse is a little more romantic than the average Analytical. Or you may find that as an Expressive, you aren't as romantic as most Expressives. The important thing is for both of you to learn what you each like, want, and need. Then you can adapt to meet each other's needs. When you do this, you will find yourself in a much happier relationship.

The best way to find out how your significant other feels about romance is to ask. Each of you could list the things that convey love and romance. Your lists will probably be quite different—not because of gender, but because of your social styles.

For Your Improvement

Reflect on the following questions and write down your answers. Refer back to them as you work toward the improvement of your personal and professional relationships.

1. Do you consider yourself more romantic or more practical?

2. Is your significant other more romantic or more practical?

3. What are some ways you can adapt to meet the needs of your significant other?

4. What are some ways your significant other can adapt to meet your needs?

5. What else have you learned from this chapter, and how could you effectively apply this information?

6

Men Retreat in Conflict, Women Advance

Mike and Alexis became increasingly frustrated as their conversation continued. The conflict started with a simple discussion about their daughter's grades and progressed to a more heated exchange about who was at fault.

"I think it would help if you quit joking about everything and started pushing Nicki to try a little harder in school. She only has three years until college, and she needs to be learning some better study skills. I feel like I'm the only one taking this seriously."

Mike responded defensively. "Look, I work with her on her assignments, and I try to make it fun. You seem to think that everything needs to be done perfectly, and I think you're just putting too much pressure on her. Nicki needs to enjoy these years. She doesn't need straight A's to get into college. You're making this into too big of a deal."

"Are you kidding me? I'm trying to equip our daughter for the real world, where it's not all fun and games like it seems to be in your little world."

"I don't think it has to be all fun and games," Mike replied. "But there needs to be some balance. If you had your way, we would all work around the clock, and no one in this house would get any time to relax, play games, or watch TV!"

Alexis wasn't convinced. "Oh, you get *plenty* of TV time while I'm getting all the chores done. I can't tell you how fun it is to work all day and then come home to see you sitting on the couch playing video games with Nicki! I can't *imagine* why that wouldn't be fun for me! I mean, come on—the dishes are piled in the sink, Nicki's homework is stacked on the table not getting done, and dinner is waiting to be made by *me*! That's a world of fun for me, Mike!"

"Maybe you could be just a little more sarcastic, Alexis. It makes you so much more attractive."

"You know what? I am done with this conversation. Why don't you just go play some video games with Nicki—that'll get her into college!" Alexis headed for the door.

"Why do you have to be so cutting?" Mike stood up and began to follow her through the room.

"Just leave me alone." Alexis grabbed her purse and keys.

"Where are you going?" Mike demanded.

"I am going to my office to finish some things. Maybe you can fix dinner for a change." As Alexis grabbed the door knob, Mike put his hand against the door.

"Why does it always have to be this way? Why can't we talk through this? You always storm off when things don't go your way, and we never end up working it out. It gets old after a while."

"A lot of things get old. I need to be done with this conversation before I say something I *won't* actually regret later. Now get your hand off the door and move!"

Mike shook his head in disgust and moved away from the door. Alexis slammed it behind her as she left the house.

> When a man sends you an impudent letter,
> sit right down and give it back to him with
> interest ten times compounded, and then
> throw both letters in the wastebasket.
> —Elbert Hubbard

How We Approach Conflict

This was a typical exchange between Mike and Alexis. They are both opinionated, outspoken people. Their responses to conflict contradict the gender stereotypes. Some experts tell us that men retreat in conflict because they are task oriented and get overwhelmed by relational issues. They also say women advance in conflict because they are so relationship oriented and need to solve the problems right away. But these gender stereotypes are just not true.

The way you respond to conflict is based more on your social style than your gender. When the pressures of interpersonal conflict rise, we tend to abandon our positive traits and resort to our negative ones. We become more extreme and rigid and less flexible and open to discussion. As a result, our interaction with others becomes counterproductive. People normally respond to conflict in four basic ways:

withdraw

control

give in

attack

You are likely to respond in one of these ways when you feel someone has put your back against the wall and is pushing your buttons. Additionally, you have a hierarchy of the four responses to conflict, and you will probably start with your primary response and work your way down the list until you find something that works. Each social style has a different hierarchy of responses, as we will see.

I dislike arguments of any kind. They are
always vulgar, and often convincing.
—Oscar Wilde

Look around at the relationships of people you know best. Ask these people how they approach conflict personally and professionally. If you look at a broad enough cross section of people, you will see that just as many women as men withdraw from conflict and just as many men as women advance. You'll discover that we respond to conflict not because of our gender, but because of our social style. Let's take a look at the ways each social style responds to conflict.

Drivers' Responses to Conflict

Drivers' first response to conflict is to take control. If they feel they are losing control, they tend to overcompensate. Drivers can become cold, unfeeling, and sarcastic. If they are mad enough, they will take a "my way or the highway" approach.

We see a good example of this in the movie *Crimson Tide* with Gene Hackman and Denzel Washington. Gene Hackman plays the Captain Frank Ramsey, commander of the nuclear submarine USS Alabama. Denzel Washington plays the second in command, Lieutenant Commander Ron Hunter. The management and conflict styles of the two differ greatly. Ramsey is the Driver. As they begin to conflict on ideas, he makes comments like this: "We're here to preserve democracy, not to practice it!" As the conflict heats up, he yells, "Mister Hunter, I've made a decision. I'm captain of this ship. Now shut the *%&# up!"

Drivers can become unbending, unyielding, and demanding in conflict. They don't like to admit they are wrong and have a hard time saying, "I'm sorry." They also need to learn how to say, "I could be wrong." That would go a long way in reducing conflict.

As you can see, Drivers' first response to conflict is to control. If that doesn't solve the conflict or relieve the tension, Drivers will likely withdraw from the situation. If that doesn't solve the conflict, they may attack those they blame for the problem. The last resort for a Driver is to give in (which you won't see very often).

If you're in conflict with Drivers, don't try to debate with them. They make great lawyers. They appreciate people who stand firm in their positions without trying to force them to change theirs. Don't escalate the conflict by telling a Driver what to do—they don't like being bossed around. (They would rather be the boss.) Try not to take them too personally because they can come across as pretty cold and unfeeling when angry.

Analyticals' Responses to Conflict

Analyticals become inflexible and nitpicky in conflict. They tend to avoid, dodge, escape, or retreat from uncomfortable situations. Drivers tend to control conflict; Analyticals tend to withdraw from it.

In the movie *Pay It Forward*, Helen Hunt plays Arlene, an alcoholic single mom working two jobs to support her son. Kevin Spacey plays Mr. Simonet, a schoolteacher who begins dating Arlene.

Mr. Simonet is a cautious Analytical who doesn't like to take risks. He has everything in order in his life and likes things just the way he has them. When relational conflict arises, Mr. Simonet withdraws. Arlene confronts him at one point in the relationship, insisting that he is trying to push her away or run away. As the conflict escalates, he withdraws. At another point in the movie, Arlene's ex shows up, posing a threat to the dating relationship between Arlene and Mr. Simonet. Instead of staying and fighting for what he wants, Mr. Simonet attempts to avoid the conflict by withdrawing. So Analyticals' first response to conflict is to withdraw. If that doesn't work, they will likely try to dominate. If that doesn't solve the conflict, they will give in to end the conflict. The last resort for an Analytical is to attack.

The difficult part in an argument is not to defend one's opinion, but rather to know it.

—André Maurois

If you're in conflict with Analyticals, don't raise your voice or become demonstrative, because they will withdraw. Speak softly and calmly and give them time to think through the issues. Sometimes they need to take a break from the conflict to analyze the options and make sure they don't lose face.

Expressives' Responses to Conflict

Expressives can become loud and obnoxious when dealing with intense personal conflict. They tend to emotionally attack others and their ideas, using condemnations and put-downs to discredit them. They have strong opinions and are quick to share them.

In the movie *A Few Good Men*, Tom Cruise plays the young and Expressive Lt. Daniel (Danny) Kaffee, an attorney for the U.S. Navy. Demi Moore plays his cocounsel, Lt. Cdr. JoAnne Galloway. Tension arises the first time they meet, and it continues as they attempt to defend two young marines who are charged with murder.

At one point during the trial, one of the key witnesses commits suicide, and the case is beginning to look bleak. JoAnne suggests to Danny that they put Col. Jessep (Jack Nicholson) on the stand and compel him to testify, a move that could implicate the colonel in the case and exonerate the two marines. However, if the colonel didn't crack on the stand, the attorneys could face legal charges for falsely accusing someone of that rank.

The conflict escalates as JoAnne tries to make her case. She pushes Danny to put Jessup on the stand and get a confession from him. Getting more and more frustrated and feeling his back against the wall, Daniel resorts to Expressive behavior and unloads on her:

"Oh! We get it from him. No problem. We just get it from him!"

Then he turns as if he is talking to the colonel on the stand and continues his rampage.

"Colonel Jessup, isn't it true that you ordered the code red on Santiago?" Then he makes a loud buzzer sound and continues.

> I'm sorry, your time's run out! What do we have for the losers, Judge? Well, for our defendants it's a lifetime at exotic Fort Leavenworth, and for defense counsel Kaffee…that's right, it's a court-martial! Yes, Johnny, after falsely accusing a highly decorated marine officer of conspiracy and perjury, Lt. Kaffee will have a long and prosperous career teaching typewriter maintenance at the Rocko Clubbo School for Women! Thank you for playing! Should we or should we not follow the advice of the galacticly stupid!

This is a perfect example of an Expressive outburst when in the midst of serious conflict. Epressives tend to lose their temper and say things they have to apologize for later.

Do not teach your children never to be
angry; teach them how to be angry.
—Lyman Abbott

In the midst of conflict, Expressives' first response is to attack. If that doesn't work, they will give in to end the conflict. We see a great example of this is in the movie *Happy Gilmore*. Adam Sandler plays Happy Gilmore. At the beginning of the movie, his girlfriend breaks up with him because he's going nowhere and she does not want to end up with a loser.

He responds by yelling, "You're a lousy kindergarten teacher. I've seen those finger paintings you bring home, and they suck!"

His girlfriend continues to leave, so he tries a different approach. "I'm sorry. I didn't mean that. They're excellent finger paintings. Please don't go."

Expressives can explode and then try to fix it. If giving in doesn't work, they will try the third tactic: domination. The last thing you will see an Expressive do is withdraw.

If you find yourself in conflict with Expressives, be prepared for a passionate exchange. Let them vent without becoming emotionally involved or getting defensive. They will eventually calm down if you don't feed their anger. Try repeating back to them what you're hearing instead of trying to address each and every point. Also, be sure not to internalize Expressives' passion or anger. When they are venting about issues and people that have nothing to do with you, you may feel as if they are yelling at you. But this is just their venting style. Take a step back and just listen if you can.

Amiables' Responses to Conflict

Amiables dislike any type of conflict so much that they will give in to avoid it. Sharing their point of view is not worth the risk of a confrontation. They would rather maintain the peace even if it hurts them. Amiables outwardly appear to agree but may be inwardly resentful. They don't want people to dislike them, and they don't want to make waves, so they give in. As a result, Amiables often harbor pent-up anger that they can't express because they hate conflict.

This is what we see in Dave Buznik (Adam Sandler) in the movie *Anger Management*. He is an Amiable executive who has a hard time letting people know what he really thinks. His boss takes advantage of his kind disposition by taking credit for his work and walking all over him. Throughout the movie, Dave encounters absolutely rude people who need someone to stand up to them, but he generally gives in to avoid the conflict. As a result, he ends up with repressed anger that comes out in the form of verbal attacks (and even a rampage with a golf club in his boss's office). If Amiables let conflict fester long enough, they will eventually stop giving in and attack instead.

So Amiables' first response is to give in. If that doesn't ease the tension or end the conflict, they will attack. If that doesn't work, they will withdraw in avoidance. The last thing you will see an Amiable do is attempt to dominate.

If a small thing has the power to make you angry,
does that not indicate something about your size?
—Sydney J. Harris

If you are in conflict with Amiables, you might notice that the tension ends quickly as they attempt to keep the peace. This doesn't make the issue go away though. Coax them to share their opinions, and provide a safe environment for them to do so. Speak softly and calmly reassure them that you really do want to hear how they feel about issues.

Also, listen carefully to Amiables' subtle ways of communicating. If Amiables very delicately offer something like, "Do you think your friend might be upset with you because of the way you responded to her?" they are probably really trying to say something like this: "You were a complete jerk to your friend, and that's why she's upset with you. Why don't you take responsibility and go apologize?" Don't listen only to what Amiables say; listen to what they don't say as well.

Survey Says

In my survey, I asked people how they responded to conflict. More men than women indicated advancing behaviors, and more women indicated withdrawing behaviors. As I mentioned earlier, more male Drivers and Expressives filled out the survey than female Drivers and Expressives, so this would make sense. Drivers and Expressives tend to advance in conflict, and Amiables and Analyticals tend to withdraw.

Whenever you're in conflict with someone,
there is one factor that can make the difference
between damaging your relationship and
deepening it. That factor is attitude.

—William James

What the Studies Show

Various studies on men and women in conflict promote the theory that women tend to make more demands in relational conflict and men tend to withdraw. Some studies have tested this hypothesis by changing the issues behind the conflict. In these scenarios, some studies showed a partial reversal in the stereotypical gender roles, and other studies showed a full reversal. I would be interested to know what the social styles were in each of the studies conducted. That may well explain the discrepancies in the outcomes.

A 1996 issue of *Journal of Marriage and Family* included a study conducted by N.A. Klinetob and D.A. Smith, which showed a complete reversal of the demand-withdraw patterns attributable to men and women when the couples were free to select their own topics of discussion for the study.

Aside from the demand-withdraw theory, other studies about gender and conflict resolution show that gender does make a difference in how we approach and resolve conflict. Still other studies and evidence show that gender makes no difference at all.

A field observation study conducted in 1989 was directed at 108 employees and managers of one organization. The employees were divided into different pairs of male/female, male/male, and female/female. They were asked to discuss whether or not their organization should adopt participatory decision making.

The gender stereotypes would dictate that men would be more assertive in their approach to resolving conflict, and women would be more friendly, cooperative, and bargaining.

The male/male pairs and the female/female pairs initially used assertiveness and reason to resolve the conflict, but the male/female pairs used reasoning and bargaining throughout the conflict resolution. The study also showed that all the pairs used friendliness at different points in time in an attempt to solve the conflict. This approach is generally attributed to women when resolving conflict, not men (Michael Papa and Elizabeth Natalle, "Gender, Strategy Selection, and Discussion Satisfaction in Interpersonal Conflict," *Western Journal of Speech Communication,* volume 53, pages 260–72).

Conflict resolution style has also been gender stereotyped by having a feminine approach to conflict resolution or a masculine approach. Some of these studies ask participants to fill out questionnaires describing themselves by selecting certain attributes. But the attributes are already gender stereotyped, so objective results are difficult to obtain.

For example, in one study, women were asked to pick certain attributes that best described them. Researchers then categorized the attributes into feminine and masculine categories to determine if women approached conflict from the feminine stereotype.

The subjects of the study were classified as masculine if they scored high on attributes like being competitive, assertive, or independent. They were classified as feminine if they scored high on attributes like being nurturing, emotional, and sensitive to others. They were classified as androgynous (neither clearly masculine or clearly feminine) if they scored high on both sets of attributes.

The study showed that women who scored high on masculine attributes employed a mostly dominating style of conflict resolution, and those who scored higher on the feminine attributes used a mostly avoidant style of conflict resolution. The researchers simply labeled a dominant conflict resolution style as masculine, labeled a nurturing style as feminine, and assumed that people who didn't fit those predetermined gender stereotypes were anomalies. They didn't understand that these ways of resolving conflict had nothing to do with gender and everything to do with social style.

A Mixed Bag

Tiffany is an Analytical, and I asked her how she responds in conflict.

"I feel stressed when I feel relationship conflict, and I tend to withdraw. I become quiet and internalize the issues. If I know someone is going to blow up at me or get too upset when talking about something, I will just not bring it up."

When I asked if she withdraws and feels a high level of stress when she has too many tasks going on at once, she laughed.

Holding on to anger is like grasping a hot coal
with the intent of throwing it at someone
else; you are the one who gets burned.

—Buddha

"Not at all. When I get things dumped on me or I have too many tasks coming at me at once, I tend to kick into gear and get them done—except when I get too many questions in a text message. I hate that! Projects don't make me feel stressed; it's the relationship stuff. I just don't like that conflict. I don't like to argue with people and be in heated discussions. Those things stress me out, not the tasks."

Tiffany's secondary social style turned out to be Driver. She excels at juggling tasks but struggles with juggling conflict in relationships. She is more task oriented than relationship oriented, and her primary social style is more introverted than extroverted. As a result, she does not advance in conflict. She withdraws, defying the gender stereotype. She also hates talking on the phone, and when men call her daily, it drives her nuts.

Tiffany is not an anomaly. Countless other Analytical and Amiable women do not advance in conflict. In fact, these two social styles hate conflict. It makes them uncomfortable and stresses them out. Driver and Expressive women do advance in conflict, as do Driver and Expressive men. They want to resolve the conflict by talking it out and debating. They are extroverts, so they naturally advance in conflict.

Conflicting Styles of Conflict Resolution

If you recall from earlier stories, Josh is Expressive and Bri is Analytical. Based on what you have read so far, who do you think advances in conflict, Bri or Josh? If you made your assumption based on gender stereotypes, your answer would probably be Bri. However, if you made your assumption based on social style, you would be correct in choosing Josh.

Bri doesn't always share when she's frustrated or upset because she doesn't want to create conflict. Josh, on the other hand, probably shares too much at times, causing Bri to feel overwhelmed with his extroverted passion about his opinions. Josh also wants things dealt with and doesn't want issues to build up or get swept under the carpet. He sees conflict as a way to work out the issues, but Bri sees conflict as a sign that things are not going well. She internalizes conflict and feels as if she is to blame somehow. She gets very quiet and initially withdraws. Josh presses in and wants to resolve problems. Josh advances in conflict, and Bri withdraws.

◀▶

The myth: Men retreat in conflict and women advance.

The truth: Expressives and Drivers tend to advance in conflict, and Amiables and Analyticals tend to withdraw.

◀▶

> After a heated argument on some trivial matter,
> Nancy Astor shouted, "If I were your wife I would put
> poison in your coffee!" Whereupon Winston Churchill
> answered, "And if I were your husband I would drink it."
> —John Fellows Akers

Examine Your Own Life

As you consider your own situation and the conflicts you regularly face, try to identify the social style of your friends, family, and coworkers. Ask yourself if you have been trying to resolve conflict according to gender stereotypes. If you have, ask yourself how that's working out for you.

If you want to be truly effective in resolving conflict, try to deal with people individually. Assessing their social style will help you know how they respond to stress and conflict and what you can do to adapt. Of course, you will need to consider other factors, including their past experience, their culture, and their developing personality. Try to approach conflict with the goal of building better relationships as you attempt to find compromise.

Analyticals	Drivers
withdraw	dominate
dominate	withdraw
give in	attack
attack	give in
Amiables	**Expressives**
give in	attack
attack	give in
withdraw	dominate
dominate	withdraw

Fig. 6A. Social styles and conflict resolution. Adapted from Robert Bolton and Dorothy G. Bolton, *Social Style / Management Style* (New York: AMACOM, 1984), 48.

For Your Improvement

Reflect on the following questions and write down your answers. Refer back to them as you work toward the improvement of your personal and professional relationships.

1. What is usually your first response to conflict: to control, withdraw, attack, or give in?

2. What is usually your significant other's first response to conflict? Your boss's? Your coworkers'?

3. How have these differences caused problems in the past?

4. What can you do to respond to conflict more effectively and help others to do the same?

5. What else have you learned from this chapter, and how could you effectively apply this information to your personal and professional life?

7

Women Are Emotional, Men Are Tough

Blake couldn't believe what he was hearing. His boss had just informed him that he would be taken off the Baron and Wesson case.

"I have been working my butt off on that case! Why in the world would you give this case to George? He doesn't even know the client!" Blake could feel the blood rushing to his face as he clenched his fists and tried to control his anger.

"Look, Blake, I think you do a great job; I really do. It's just that the principal of the firm isn't connecting with you. He feels overwhelmed by your approach. Maybe you're just a little too passionate for him. Try not to take it so personally."

"How can I not take it personally?" Blake shot back at his boss. "You're telling me it's because of me. What exactly did I do to offend this guy?"

His boss motioned for Blake to have a seat. "It's nothing specific, Blake. He's just a quiet guy who seems to be pretty antisocial. He struggles with people who come on strong, and he's not comfortable with people who show their emotions."

"Are you kidding me? You would think this guy would appreciate someone who is real. I have been nothing but up-front, honest, and transparent with him. If I came on too strong, it's only because I was passionate about what I believe, and I believe that our services fit the needs of his firm and that he needs to make some changes!"

"I hear you Blake," his boss responded with a deep sigh. "Again, you do a great job, and yes, you are passionate. I appreciate that. But some people struggle with that passion and take it the wrong way. Let's get you focused on another case and put this one behind us."

> Human behavior flows from three main
> sources: desire, emotion, and knowledge.
> —Plato

"Whatever." Blake stood up and started for the door. "It's this kind of crap that makes it hard for me to put everything I've got into this job!" He slammed the door behind him and stormed to his office, fighting back the flood of emotions that were rushing to the surface.

Blake is not an abnormal guy who happens to struggle with a lot of emotions. He's an Expressive. The client who didn't want to work with Blake was an Analytical. Analyticals have a difficult time with demonstrative and emotional people. Drivers also struggle with people who are emotional, and they have an even harder time dealing with people who are overly sensitive.

> I'm a sensitive guy. If you are a woman and
> you're in any kind of emotional duress and you
> write a song about it, I'll buy your album.
> —Matthew Perry

The gender stereotype tells us that women are emotional and men are tough. Men don't cry or wear their hearts on their sleeves. Men are tough as nails and don't feel the emotions that women feel. The myth goes on to describe women as thin-skinned and emotional. They don't have a problem crying at the drop of a hat, and they always wear their hearts on their sleeves. The truth is, Amiables and Expressives tend to share their emotions freely, and Drivers and Analyticals tend to be less emotionally expressive.

The Hormone Factor

Before I go any further on this topic, I do want to address one issue that affects this gender stereotype: hormones. When a woman has PMS, is going through menopause, or is experiencing hormonal fluctuations in pregnancy, she may be much more prone to tears and overwhelming emotions than she usually would be.

A Driver or Analytical woman is normally not an emotional creature. She doesn't cry easily and tends to look at things matter-of-factly. However, if she is dealing with a hormonal issue, she may find herself more emotional than usual. But setting aside hormones, an Amiable or Expressive is normally more apt to feel and share emotions; a Driver or Analytical is not.

Emotional Versus Sensitive

Women have been tagged with the stereotype of being sensitive. This label is sometimes used positively and sometimes negatively.

Being emotional and being sensitive are two different things. Amiables and Expressives don't mind showing their emotions, and Amiables can be overly sensitive about their feelings. Expressives, on the other hand, can be insensitive, like Drivers. Analyticals can also be overly sensitive, like Amiables.

We meet a woman who is both insensitive and unemotional in the movie *Jerry Maguire*. In this movie, Tom Cruise plays Jerry Maguire, an Expressive sports agent. Kelly Preston plays his girlfriend, Avery Bishop. Avery is a hard-core Driver. Jerry was supposed to get a contract signed by the number one draft pick in the NFL. Instead, being the Expressive, relationship-oriented type, he takes a handshake from the player's father. The night before the draft the football player signs with another agent, and Jerry is left out in the cold with only one client left.

◀▶

The myth: Women are sensitive, men are insensitive.

The truth: Amiables and Analyticals are generally sensitive, and Drivers and Expressives can be insensitive.

◀▶

He returns from a long trip to break the bad news to Avery. He's hoping for some sensitivity from his girlfriend, but what he gets is a royal shredding for not getting the contract signed. When he tells her she's adding to his nightmare, she reminds him of their deal when they first got together: "Brutal truth."

Jerry responds by saying "I think *you* added the brutal."

Avery lets out a sarcastic laugh and responds with this:

> Jerry, some people have that sensitivity thing. I don't have it. I don't cry at movies, I don't gush over babies, I don't celebrate Christmas five months early, and I'm not about to tell the man who just ruined both our lives, "Oh, poor baby." That's me, for better or worse. But I do love you.

That is a typical Driver in the midst of conflict—unemotional, cold, unfeeling, and matter-of-fact. Male or female, the tough side of the Driver will emerge.

Survey Says

In my survey, I asked people if they were more likely to be accused of being too sensitive or too insensitive. According to gender stereotypes, more men than women should have responded that they are accused of being insensitive, and more women than men should have responded that they were more likely to be accused of being too sensitive.

The survey results fell in line with the gender stereotype. More men than women said they were more likely to be accused of being too insensitive, and more women than men said they were more likely to be accused of being too sensitive. So if we left it at that, one might conclude that our research solidifies the gender stereotype. But not so fast. When we break it down further and cross-reference social style, we can begin to understand and interpret the responses more accurately.

It is not because the truth is too difficult to see that we make mistakes...we make mistakes because the easiest and most comfortable course for us is to seek insight where it accords with our emotions, especially selfish ones.
—Alexander Solzhenitsyn

The more insensitive social styles are the Drivers and Expressives. The more sensitive social styles are the Amiables and the Analyticals. Of the men who responded to the survey, the vast majority who said they were more insensitive were Drivers and Expressives. The vast majority of men who responded by saying they were more likely to be accused of being too sensitive were Amiables and Analyticals. This pattern proved to be true for the female respondents as well.

More male Drivers and Expressives than female Amiables and Analyticals responded to the survey. This would account for more men stating that they were more likely to be accused of being too insensitive. When we remove the gender of the respondents, the survey results show that Drivers and Expressives tend to be more insensitive, and Amiables and Analyticals tend to be more sensitive

When you stop examining behavior based on gender and instead look at social style, the patterns of behavior begin to make more sense. General sensitivity is not a gender issue; it's a social-style issue.

Other Research

Erina MacGeorge has conducted research on gender issues and has had numerous articles published in various academic journals, including *Sex Roles: A Journal of Research.*

MacGeorge discovered what I assert: Men and women tend to have a pretty even level of sensitivity and regard to personal relationships. Mac-George didn't go so far as to attribute the differences to social style, but the results of the study are interesting nonetheless.

Often, the less there is to justify a traditional custom, the harder it is to get rid of it.
—Mark Twain

The research showed that men and women both liked to express sensitivity when it came to their friends' problems. It also showed a pretty even number of men to women who liked to express sympathy toward others. Additionally, the research showed that both men and women did not like any form of comforting that dismissed or made light of their problems (stereotypically a male style) and preferred comforting that validated their feelings and perspectives (stereotypically a female style). The research showed that men valued empathy and warmth as much as women did.

Some of the research showed a slight difference in results. One example showed that more men than women were likely to give advice to solve problems where more women than men were likely to be supportive and offer help. The difference in results here was only 2 percent, which is minimal. I will go out on a limb here and say that if MacGeorge had cross-referenced the results with social style, it is likely that more male Drivers and Analyticals responded to the survey than female. This would account for the differences in responses that actually do conform to the gender stereotypes.

The Cultural Factor

Contemporary Western culture reinforces an expectation for boys and men to be tough. Both fathers and mothers project this expectation in early ages as boys repeatedly hear, "Boys don't cry," "Get tough," "Don't act like a sissy," or "You're acting like a little girl." Boys quickly learn that showing softness or emotion will only get them chastised somehow.

Parents are not the only ones to blame. Friends will mock boys for being too sensitive. Women expect men to be strong and tough but also want them to be soft and sensitive. No wonder men are so confused about this issue!

The media create an expectation of toughness for men. The box office is filled with action-packed, heroic movies with men who are tough and who show very little emotion (other than anger). Video games portray the same image and are increasingly violent, sending a signal to boys that being mean and tough is where it's at.

Even some of the most well-intentioned experts and authors paint this image of men as tough and wild. Some claim that all men are born with the heart of a warrior, wanting constant risk and adventure in their lives. The more introverted and sensitive men find themselves feeling less like men as they fall short of these expectations. They try to hide their fears and insecurities, afraid they may be found out. They don't know that millions of other men are just as sensitive, emotional, and tenderhearted as they are and that they are also real men.

The cultural stereotype of male toughness is hurting our young boys who become confused men. They don't know how to express their emotions in a socially acceptable way and still be considered a man's man.

Our culture reinforces a stereotype that girls are soft, sweet, and emotional. Maybe you recall this nursery rhyme:

> What are little boys made of?
> Snips and snails and puppy-dogs' tails,
> That's what little boys are made of.
> What are little girls made of?
> Sugar and spice, and everything nice.
> That's what little girls are made of.

I heard that rhyme growing up, and so did everyone I know. Countless girls wonder what might be wrong with them when they don't feel so sweet and emotional and when they love playing with frogs and bugs. Society tells them they are too emotional to handle a man's job, and they grow up selling themselves short.

Women who don't feel or express much emotion as adults are often chastised for being cold and heartless. They struggle under a cultural expectation that women are sensitive and emotional and men are more insensitive and unemotional. Helping people to understand social style at a young age would help address some of these cultural issues that are feeding gender stereotypes.

Interviews with 30 Male Firefighters

When you think of a male firefighter, what comes to mind? If you are like most people, you picture a buff and tough risk taker who epitomizes the man's man stereotype.

I read a fire-service magazine article that claimed that all firefighters had the same personality style. They were all type A, bungee-jumping adrenaline junkies who loved to run into burning buildings, and that's why they joined the fire service. This would make all firefighters either Drivers or Expressives.

But of course, firefighters don't spend all of their time running into burning buildings. In fact, across the Unites States, career firefighters spend an average of only 4 percent of their time on emergency calls, and only 1 percent of that is on fire suppression. Firefighters are the first responders to more than 70 percent of all 911 medical emergency calls. Firefighters do a lot more than just fight fires.

The degree of one's emotions varies inversely
with one's knowledge of the facts.
—Bertrand Russell

Not all firefighters are type A risk takers. Yes, they take risks, but that doesn't necessarily come naturally or easily to every firefighter. I have conducted social style analyses on thousands of firefighters in hundreds of fire departments across the United States, and I have found just as many Amiables and Analyticals as Drivers and Expressives. All four social styles are represented in both male and female firefighters in fire departments all over the country (although the fire service is still predominately male).

The idea that all male firefighters are emotionally tough intrigued me. So I conducted interviews on 30 male firefighters from all over the United States. I asked the firefighters several series of questions, and their responses may surprise you.

The first series of questions I asked allowed me to determine the social style of each firefighter. All four social styles were represented. Not surprisingly, the Drivers and Expressives offered a lot more information than I asked for, and I had to prod the Amiables and Analyticals a little more.

I asked whether the firefighter considered himself to be a big risk taker. The Drivers and Expressives were quick to respond with a resounding *yes!* The Amiables and Analyticals were reluctant in their answers, but after reassuring them that the interviews were confidential, they confided that they were not big risk takers and would not engage in extreme activities like bungee jumping.

I also asked whether the firefighter ever had his feelings hurt at work by another firefighter. The Drivers adamantly answered no.

Pure logic is the ruin of the spirit.

—Antoine de Saint-Exupery

One Driver firefighter actually stated, "This job requires a thick skin. You can't let people get to you or hurt your feelings. You can't be sensitive and be a firefighter—you will never survive."

I then asked him if he thought women were more sensitive than men. He said he thought they were. I then asked how he felt about women in the fire service. He replied, "I have no problem with it as long as they can physically do the job. I work with one tough cookie who can run circles around some of our male firefighters." I asked if he thought she was sensitive, and he replied, "Nope. She's not like a normal girl in that way. In fact, she's a lot like me."

He started to realize he was tangled up in a gender stereotype, and when it didn't fit, he simply dismissed a less sensitive woman as abnormal. But in reality, she was most likely a Driver, just like him.

When I asked one of the Amiables if he had ever had his feelings hurt at work he said, "Many times. I would never let the guys know about it, though, or I would never hear the end of it!" Interestingly enough, most of the other

Amiables and Analyticals had similar responses. They didn't want to deal with conflict, and they didn't want the other firefighters in the station to know that their feelings had been hurt. As a result, most of the Driver and Expressive firefighters just assume that all firefighters are emotionally tough and don't have hurt feelings. Interesting.

First Impressions Can Be Misleading

When I first met Brandon, I was a little overwhelmed by his size. He must have been six feet six and 230 pounds. His hands and arms were massive. I felt as if I'd met a representative of World Wrestling Entertainment. I could just imagine him leaping off of the top rope of a wrestling ring and smashing somebody.

Our tendency to sometimes let our imaginations run wild is amazing. Our first impression of people is not always accurate. This was true with Brandon and me. At first glance, you would think he was a construction worker, a policeman, or maybe a linebacker on a football team. I was caught off guard when I found out he was a second-grade schoolteacher.

He was not a rough and tough, "push people around" kind of guy. He was a compulsive talker, humorous, and prone to exaggeration. He was a combination of Robin Williams and Jim Carrey—a true Expressive.

He was restless and had a hard time sitting still during our conversation. He waved his arms around as he talked and had extremely animated facial expressions. He had no problem sharing his emotions, and they varied a great deal.

You could see an excitement and sparkle in his eyes as he talked about his second-grade students. And then his face would suddenly become serious. He wanted to know how he could overcome his lack of discipline. He knew he had a procrastination problem. He disliked details, deadlines, and nitpicky administrators. He was overly relaxed about being on time and would often forget obligations. He struggled with a rebellious spirit with regard to his superiors.

His mile-a-minute talking continued with a joke about principals. Then he turned serious again, and his tone carried a touch of anger. He didn't think that administrators had any idea what went on in the classroom. He thought they were simply out of touch.

As he talked and talked, I listened carefully and smiled inside. I was smiling for two reasons. First, he talked so fast, I could barely get a word in edgewise. Second, he clearly broke the stereotype of emotional women and tough men. Sitting in front of me was living proof that some men are highly emotional and not as tough as they seem.

Brandon could carry on a conversation with anyone, even total strangers. He had no reservations about sharing his emotions, whether happiness, sadness, fear, or anger. Brandon was highly emotional and somewhat unpredictable.

Ashley, on the other hand, was quite different. She was certainly not emotional. She was all business. She was definitely a bottom-line woman. Ashley had no time for extended stories, long explanations, or expanded excuses.

She could multitask with her eyes closed. No one would accuse her of being lazy or forgetful. In fact, Ashley did not take time to slow down in any area of her life. The word *relax* was not in her dictionary.

That is one reason she stopped in to talk. Her high energy threatened those who could not keep pace with her. Her impatience and sarcasm were damaging relationships at home and at work. She was demanding of herself and of everyone else, and they didn't like it.

By starving emotions we become humorless, rigid
and stereotyped; by repressing them we become
literal, reformatory and holier-than-thou; encouraged,
they perfume life; discouraged, they poison it.
—Joseph Collins

People around the office nicknamed Ashley "Lucy" because she picked on people the way Lucy picks on Charlie Brown. Ashley was inflexible, demanding, and highly opinionated. Some of the other employees thought she was like an American Margaret Thatcher, willing to confront and take on anyone who disagreed with her opinions.

Like Lucy of *Peanuts* fame, Ashley did display one emotion: anger under stress. And Ashley seemed to be stressed a great deal of the time.

Ashley's story was like the story of the pastor who played golf with one of his deacons. When the deacon hit his ball into the rough, he swore up a storm. When the pastor hit his ball into the rough, he said nothing. When the deacon hit his ball into the water hole, he swore like a trooper. When the pastor hit his ball into the water hole, he didn't speak a word. When the deacon hit his ball into the sand trap, he cursed for several minutes. When the pastor hit his ball into the sand trap, he didn't respond at all.

Finally, the deacon said to the pastor, "I really admire you. You don't say anything or show any emotion when your ball goes into the rough, the water hole, or the sand trap. I have a problem with swearing when that happens to me."

"That's true," said the pastor. "I don't swear, but where I spit, the grass dies."

Ashley seems very unemotional and businesslike, but wherever she spits out impatient, sarcastic, and negative comments, she kills relationships.

Ashley, like many women, can make quick decisions and show great initiative. She is a natural leader and has a take-charge attitude. However, not everyone appreciates Ashley's tough and unfeeling demeanor. Her husband and children are beginning to think Hitler was reincarnated in Ashley. She has developed the reputation of being as hard as nails.

Drivers have plenty of positive qualities. Regardless of gender, they are often productive, visionary, and courageous, and they can attract followers. They can also be optimistic, practical, and decisive.

Unfortunately, Ashley was displaying the Driver's negative traits: pushiness, insensitivity, and severity. People around her did not appreciate her harsh, opinionated, and unsympathetic spirit. Her domineering and proud actions created the image of her being hard, uncaring, and tough. Ashley wanted to change that picture.

Brandon and Ashley were not experiencing gender role reversals, regardless of what many experts may claim. Instead, they were experiencing the reality of their differing social styles. The idea that men are tough and women are emotional is a stereotype that continues to confuse and frustrate people who don't fit the mold.

Breaking the Cycle

You don't have to be a genius to see that boys are more emotional when they are younger and desensitize as they get older. You have undoubtedly also noticed that some boys are more tenderhearted and sensitive than others.

Social styles emerge at a young age. My goal is to educate parents, teachers, and children that it is perfectly normal for some boys to be emotional and some to be more unemotional. We also need to make sure girls understand that it is perfectly normal for some girls to be more emotional and some to be less so. The important thing is to help children and adults understand their social style and notice where they need to grow.

For Your Improvement

Reflect on the following questions and write down your answers. Refer back to them as you work toward the improvement of your personal and professional relationships.

1. Do you tend to show little emotion or show a lot of emotion?

2. How do you feel around people who show their emotions much more freely or much less freely than you share yours?

3. What else have you learned from this chapter, and how could you effectively apply this information to your personal and professional life?

8

Men Need Accomplishments, Women Need Relationships

The media offer countless depictions of men who are driven to achieve, to accomplish, to conquer. They present women as focused on more and better relationships. Even if a woman is portrayed in a working environment, she is still tagged with the innate need for relationship over accomplishment, which some experts try to use to explain why more men than women hold managerial positions. The argument is that women are just not task oriented enough because their focus is settled too narrowly on relationships.

This stereotype carries over into the home as well. Many experts insist that when a man comes home from work, he is still focused on tasks, not relationships. His wife is portrayed as pacing near the front door, just waiting for him to get home so she can engage in her much-needed relationship communication. If she's a stay-at-home mom, she gets her daytime fix from her friends and community groups. If she's a career woman, that fix comes from her coworkers, whom she will innately attempt to bond with. Her need for relationship does not stop at the end of the day, however. When her man comes home, she still needs to share every detail of her day with him because her life revolves around relationships—or so the stereotype would have you believe.

Because I am a woman, I must make unusual efforts to succeed. If I fail, no one will say, "She doesn't have what it takes." They will say, "Women don't have what it takes."
—Clare Boothe Luce

Plenty of women would probably want to vomit if they read this. Just as many men would scratch their heads, wondering what's wrong with them if the need for accomplishment doesn't drive their every decision. These stereotypes just don't fit a lot of people, and they need to be dispelled.

Perpetuating the Stereotype

A 2008 study published in the June issue of *Journal of Broadcasting & Electronic Media* revealed the prevalence of this stereotype in prime-time television shows. The study examined 124 prime-time television programs shown on six different networks. Male and female social roles were examined to determine if stereotyping was occurring.

Not surprisingly, the vast majority of female characters in these shows were depicted in interpersonal roles that encompassed romance, family, and friends. Women were mostly portrayed as being driven primarily by relationship issues.

The male characters engaged in sharply contrasting roles. The men were shown more often in work-related roles and scenarios instead of interpersonal roles, thus perpetuating the stereotype that men need accomplishment and women need relationship.

Another study conducted in 2009 and published in *Sex Roles* examined 205 college students' perceptions of other students who come back to school after having a child. Participants were asked questions about women who choose to continue their education shortly after the birth of a child. All of the participants perceived this choice to be less feminine, more dominant, more arrogant, more coldhearted, and less warm than a mother's decision to discontinue her education.

A relationship is a living thing. It needs and benefits from the same attention to detail that an artist lavishes on his art.
—David Viscott

The Truth of the Matter

The truth is, having an innate drive toward accomplishment or relationship is not about gender, it's about social style. It's the difference between being task oriented or relationship oriented. The task-oriented person is much more focused on getting things accomplished than the relationship-oriented person.

Drivers are task oriented and extraverted. They are born to achieve and gravitate toward leadership positions and constant accomplishment. Regardless of whether they are male or female, Drivers are more likely to become workaholics than are the other social styles. They want to accomplish things quickly so they can move on to the next task. They prefer speed over accuracy and are not great with the details. They are determined to follow through on their goals and are the most productive people on earth. Drivers become restless at work and at home if they don't feel productive.

Analyticals are also more task oriented than relationship oriented, but they are not as ambitious as Drivers. They prefer accuracy over speed and are great with the details. Whether at work or at home, they will find projects to accomplish and take great pride in the quality of their work. Female Analyticals are just as task focused as their male counterparts.

Amiables need relationships much more than they need accomplishments. They are not prone to ambition and often need encouragement when setting goals. They focus a great deal of their time on building positive relationships and minimizing conflict. Male Amiables are just as concerned about other people's feelings as female Amiables are.

Expressives can be ambitious, but they don't always follow through on projects or work hard to reach high goals. They are much more relationship oriented than Drivers and want to have fun in life. Socializing is much more important to an Expressive than accomplishment. A male Expressive can be just as relationship driven as a female.

Real-Life Scenarios

Maybe you are familiar with couples who fit the stereotypes we are discussing. The man appears to be married to his job rather than his wife. He works late and is driven to achieve in everything he does. His identity appears to be built on the goals he achieves and the things he accomplishes. His wife often complains to her friends that he doesn't spend enough time with her and the kids. He never seems to want to talk about the little things in life. He appears preoccupied and restless most of the time. Some people would look at this scenario and say, "Typical male," which would be an inaccurate stereotype. The correct assumption would be, "Typical Driver."

Think about other people you know. Plenty of couples live the stereotype in reverse. The woman gains her sense of identity from her career. She works long hours and is constantly striving for the next promotion. She gets involved in local politics and commits herself to more boards, committees, and projects than she has time for. Her husband complains that he doesn't see her enough and that they don't spend enough quality time together. Some experts would call this a role reversal, which perpetuates the stereotype that normal men need accomplishment and normal women need relationship.

There's only one corner of the universe you can be certain of improving, and that's your own self.
—Aldous Huxley

Countless men and women have found themselves utterly frustrated with these stereotypes as they wonder what must be wrong with them when their lives don't align with these myths. Plenty of men find themselves needing relationship more than accomplishment, and plenty of women find themselves needing accomplishment more than relationship.

Domestic Godesses Can Be Drivers

Some Driver and Analytical women choose to not work outside the home. This does not necessarily mean they are less focused on accomplishments. What they strive to accomplish is just different from what a career-oriented Driver or Analytical sets her sights on. The stay-at-home Analytical will focus on tasks and keeping a very clean and orderly home. She will have systems of efficiency, high standards, and opinions about how to do things correctly.

The Driver mom will exercise a somewhat strict parenting style and will be accomplishment driven as well. She will just be much more outspoken than the Analytical. The Driver will also push her children to achieve and accomplish, which can create significant conflict if the children value relationships more than tasks.

Achievement, Goals, Marriage, and Commitment

Catherine Mosher of Duke Medical Center and Sharon Danoff-Burg of the University of Albany conducted a study of 80 men and 157 women. Among other things, the study examined participants' willingness to sacrifice achievement goals for romantic relationships.

The study showed that both men and women showed strong desires for individual achievement as well as relationship intimacy. One finding was unexpected: Men were more likely than women to give up their achievement goals for the priority of a romantic relationship. This study challenges the stereotypes and assumptions that women put people and relationships ahead of the need for achievement while men have a greater need for achievement than relationship.

Another study dispels the myth that women push for marriage and men run from commitment. A study published in 2008 in *Gender Roles* showed that when unmarried couples had a child together, the woman was more likely to retreat from the idea of marriage than the man.

Another 2008 study published in *Sex Roles* dispels the gender stereotype that men are more committed to paid employment than women because of their innate drive toward accomplishment. The study revealed that women were just as committed to paid employment as men. Although the study did not address the social-style issue, the need for accomplishment will not follow gender; it will follow social style.

Survey Says

In my survey, I asked respondents to answer true or false to the following statement: You are often accused of being too independent ("you don't need anyone!"). The responses did not follow the typical gender stereotype. Instead, most Drivers and Analyticals responded true, while most Amiables and Expressives responded false.

> To accomplish great things we must not only act,
> but also dream; not only plan, but also believe.
> —Anatole France

I also asked respondents whether they tended to focus on building relationships or completing tasks. Drivers and Analyticals mostly responded that they focus on completing tasks, while Amiables and Expressives mostly responded that they focus on building relationships, regardless of their gender.

Live for Tomorrow, Live for Today

Owen was not a task-oriented and detailed guy. He preferred not to be out in front of groups but liked to contribute behind the scenes. He could lead a group of people if he had to, but he tried never to get in that position.

He didn't have driving urges to go into higher education and get some kind of degree or to get ahead financially and purchase toys like fast cars, big houses, or motorboats. The thought of climbing the corporate ladder had no appeal to him. He was completely content to live a simple life. Enjoying a quiet time at home, playing with his kids, and watching movies with his wife were highlights to him. Relationships were more important to him than goals and accomplishments.

Owen was content to live like Winnie the Pooh, who doesn't get ruffled by many things in life. He was perfectly content to be a follower. Letting other people make decisions seemed like the polite and diplomatic thing to do.

Owen's relaxed lifestyle worked well except for one thing. He was married to Madison, who was a real go-getter and a detailed woman. She performed tasks with deliberation and wanted things done correctly the first time. That was not exactly how Owen viewed life.

Owen liked to please everyone, especially Madison. This caused some conflict because she had very high standards and was often hard to please. Madison was detailed oriented, and Owen was laid-back. Madison liked everything done just so. Owen had never been able to figure out what "just so" was. He tried to put the decorator pillows on their bed the way she did, but it never really happened. He always saw her move them a little this way or that. He just sighed and walked away.

When Madison asked Owen to do some tasks around the house, he sincerely planned to do them after he finished what he was doing. Yet she would be upset with him when he didn't drop everything and do the tasks immediately. Madison made lists, schedules, and plans for most of her activities and for the activities of her family members. Sometimes the family was not even aware of all of these tasks and plans. Of course, conflict naturally occurred as a result.

Owen and the children viewed Madison like Mr. Spock from *Star Trek*. Spock was organized, detailed, and often critical. He loved facts and perfection. Madison liked to plan in advance for trips and vacations. Owen liked to do things on the spur of the moment. Madison was not excited about going to parties and being with a lot of people. Owen liked to be with a group and interact with different personalities.

Never be satisfied with what you achieve,
because it all pales in comparison with what
you are capable of doing in the future.
—Rabbi Nochem Kaplan

The biggest rub in Owen and Madison's relationship had to do with their differing priorities. Madison's first priority was to accomplish tasks and get things done. Her motto would be, "Plan for the future." Owen felt that tasks were necessary but that the most important thing in life was developing lasting relationships. He would respond to Madison by saying, "Live for today." The constant rub in their relationship was the difference between tasks and relationships as shown below:

Madison tended to…	*Owen tended to…*
value logic	value sentiment
question conclusions	accept conclusions
guard emotions	unload emotions
be firm	be sympathetic
be restless	be contented
organize	be free
think Owen was out of touch	think Madison was missing out

The differences between Owen and Madison were not gender issues. They were social-style issues. Madison was Analytical, and Owen was more Amiable. The key for them to survive each other was to learn to appreciate each other's positives and not focus on the negatives.

This did not happen right away for a number of reasons. The children began to side with Owen because he was more fun and less strict than their mother. Owen secretly liked the fact that the children were on his side. This continued until Owen began to see that the children were using him to get what they wanted. He also realized that he and Madison were not providing the stability and security of a unified position on important subjects. Owen began to change his viewpoint and to move closer to Madison's logical and careful thinking. Madison deeply appreciated that. She began to stop seeing herself as a lone voice crying in the wilderness. She also began to realize that some of her demands were out of line and too legalistic. As a result, harmony began to emerge from a formerly dysfunctional discipline system.

Madison also began to back off from making so many lists for her family. Owen in turn responded positively to the release of nagging pressure. He began to respond more quickly to her needs without being asked repeatedly. Madison began to realize that Owen needed to be involved in parties and social gatherings even though she was a little uncomfortable. She actually began to put parties on her list of things to do!

Owen began to realize that dealing with people and groups was an emotional drain for Madison. He saw that accomplishing some tasks energized her and that helped her handle being exposed to more relationships.

Madison came to understand that just the opposite was true for Owen. Tasks drained him, and people energized him. With this insight, she began to help plan opportunities for Owen to go out with the boys and have some fun. Before long, she could see that she had a much happier man to live with.

Understanding and Compromise

Owen and Madison demonstrate that cohesive relationships emerge from understanding and compromise. The first step is to understand social style. When you move away from gender stereotypes and examine the social style of your loved ones, you can see what drives them: either task and accomplishment or building relationships.

Once you understand people's social styles, you can discover their differing priorities. That's when it's time for compromise. Learning to adapt to meet the needs of others is a critical skill in developing maturity and learning to live peacefully with them.

Drivers and Analyticals need to lighten up a little on the task lists, learn to relax, and have more fun to accommodate their Expressive and Amiable counterparts. Expressives and Amiables need to compromise for the Drivers and Analyticals by stepping up and getting the things done that need to get done.

Take inventory of the people you live and work with. Determine whether they tend to be driven by tasks or by relationships. Compare this with your own style and start thinking about ways to be more understanding and to compromise.

Virtue knows that it is impossible to get on without compromise, and tunes herself, as it were, a trifle sharp to allow for an inevitable fall in playing.
—Samuel Butler

Analytical	Driver
tasks are primary	tasks are primary
relationships are secondary	relationships are secondary
need for accomplishment	need for accomplishment
focus on projects	focus on projects
priority: quality	priority: speed
Amiable	**Expressive**
relationships are primary	relationships are primary
tasks are secondary	tasks are secondary
need for connectedness	need for connectedness
focus on people	focus on people
priority: kindness	priority: socializing

Fig. 8A. Social styles, tasks, and relationships.

For Your Improvement

Reflect on the following questions and write down your answers. Refer back to them as you work toward the improvement of your personal and professional relationships.

1. Is your identity determined more by your sense of accomplishment or your relationships?

2. How does this affect your relationships with the people you live and work with?

3. How can you start to adapt to be more balanced between tasks and relationships?

4. What else have you learned from this chapter, and how could you effectively apply this information to your personal and professional life?

9

Men Are Thinkers,
Women Are Feelers

M ost people are keenly aware of these gender stereotypes:

Men use their heads; women use their hearts.

Men are better thinkers; women are better feelers.

Men base decisions on facts; women base decisions on emotion.

Men are biologically equipped to think; women are biologically equipped to feel.

Men think through issues; women feel through them.

Men are logical; women are intuitive.

All of these gender stereotypes characterize men as problem solvers and women as communicators. But these assumptions share one very big problem—men *aren't* better problem solvers, and women *aren't* better communicators. Let's examine some of these stereotypes and look at the more important issue of social style.

That Corpus Callosum

A sweeping generalization claims that women are sympathizers and men are systemizers. Much of this is allegedly supported by studies of the brain that seek to explain why women have more empathy and can multitask and why men are poor listeners but good at detail. The problem starts with the assumption that these gender stereotypes are actually true. Once researchers make that assumption, they set out to figure out why men and women act that way.

> A thick head can do as much damage as a hard heart.
> —H.W. Dodds

These studies state that parts of women's corpus callosum—a band of fibers that connect the right and left sides of the brain—may be thicker than men's. These findings are followed by claims like "This *may* explain why women are better at..." or "This *may* explain why men don't...." making the assumption that the initial generalization is correct.

Here's a news flash that doesn't make the headlines like the gender myths do: Most researchers will admit that much greater neurological differences exist between individuals in general than between men and women in particular. One person may have three times as many nerve fibers in the corpus callosum as another person, regardless of gender. If we dissected these brains with a focus on social style instead of gender, we might discover that those threefold corpus callosum brains belonged to Drivers, and that could be the reason they are so thick-headed!

All humor aside, no one has examined the brain in relation to social style. Studies have focused only on gender, and the unknowns and inconsistencies are too numerous to ignore. The first step in the right direction for all researchers would be to lay down the gender stereotypes and start examining differences in people based on social style.

Chess, Jobs, and Intellectual Capacity

If both men and women are capable of the same levels of thinking capacity, why do more men dominate high-level thinking fields? One study published in the August 2006 issue of *Sex Roles* called into question the claims that occupational stereotypes are actually diminishing. This study showed that people still associate more analytical jobs (such as engineers and accountants) with men, and they associate more relationship or feeling-oriented jobs (such as teachers and caregivers) with women. This could play a critical factor in how people view the suitability of jobs based on their gender. Many women have been convinced that they simply lack the biological makeup to make the grade in a high-level thinking job.

Let's look at the game of chess as an example. This is considered one of the most mentally challenging games, requiring a lot of analytical skill and thinking.

We should take care not to make the intellect our god;
it has, of course, powerful muscles, but no personality.
—Albert Einstein

The *European Journal of Social Psychology* published a study in March 2008 examining why women are so underrepresented in the world of chess. Only 5 percent of the registered tournament players worldwide are women. Only 1 percent of the grand masters (the highest title a chess player can obtain aside from world champion) are women. The study argues that gender stereotypes are responsible.

The study paired 42 male and female players according to their ability. The players engaged in online chess games. When the players were unaware of the gender of their opponents, the women played just as well as the men. When the gender stereotype was activated and the women were aware that they were up against a man, a drastic drop in performance resulted. When they were falsely told they were playing against a woman (but they were actually playing against a man), they performed at the same level as their male opponents. The preconditioned stereotype that men are better thinkers than women can actually cause women to perform at lower levels.

Plenty of studies show that gender is not an adequate predictor of achievement, academic skill level, or emotional tendencies. Many studies related to math skills for boys and girls have shown that the similarities overshadow the differences. Unfortunately, many researchers are looking only for differences, and as a result, they either miss or completely ignore the similarities.

Thinkers and Feelers

If you consider some of the greatest geniuses throughout history (both male and female), you will notice a lot of Analyticals represented. Of course, not all Analyticals are geniuses, but they are certainly more genius-prone than the rest of us with Driver, Expressive, and Amiable social styles. Analyticals don't always use this thinking capacity, but both males and females can have it.

That's not to say that the other three social styles cannot be incredibly intelligent people, because they can. But your tendency to look at life and make decisions according to a rational thinking process or according to your feelings is determined by your social style, not your gender.

Drivers and Analyticals tend to make decisions aside from emotions or feelings. In fact, they often become uncomfortable if someone around them regularly shows a lot of emotion. They struggle with people who don't use logic or reasoning to make decisions.

If you make people think they're thinking, they'll love you; but if you really make them think, they'll hate you.
—Don Marquis

Amiables and Expressives pay much more attention to their feelings, and they will often show them. As it becomes more and more socially acceptable for men to show their emotions, we are starting to see more and more Expressive and Amiable men coming out of the emotional closet. Amiables and Expressives often view Drivers and Analyticals as a little on the cold and unfeeling side and wish they would show more emotion and feelings.

Serendipity

Clayton and Hannah joined my wife, me, and two other couples for a barbecue in a park. I smiled inside as I watched them describe their recent vacation.

Clayton could hardly contain himself as he pulled out a stack of pictures and began to show the group. "Hey, look at these beauties," he began as he raised his voice to grab everyone's attention.

I could see that Hannah was not excited at what Clayton was doing. "Oh, I don't think everyone is interested in those pictures," she said.

"Yeah, they'll love them," he said while nodding his head up and down, looking for approval from his friends. "Look at this one. It's a picture of us with a flat tire on the freeway." Clayton laughed as he passed it around.

Hannah responded by saying, "I asked Clayton to check our spare tire before we left to see if it had enough air in it. He forgot. It was also flat."

"That's what we have AAA towing for!" replied Clayton as he laughed again and passed around another picture.

Hannah turned to one of the other wives. "He never plans ahead. It's a good thing I brought a map and marked our route, or we would have gotten lost. Clayton just jumped into the car and said, 'Let's have an adventure.' I asked him if he loaded all the children's luggage in the car. He said, 'Sure!' I then pointed to two bags by the garage door and said, 'What are those?' He said, 'Oh.' He's so forgetful."

The brain is a wonderful organ; it starts working
the moment you get up in the morning and
does not stop until you get into the office.
—Robert Frost

"I leave all those details to Hannah," Clayton said as he overheard the conversation. "She's the organized one. She's got lists and lists of what we are going to do and see on the vacation. In fact, almost each moment of our day was planned. I like a little more unpredictability and living by the moment. It's fun to have serendipity now and then."

"What's serendipity?" asked one of the other husbands.

That was all Clayton needed. He was off and running.

"My favorite new word. I think it was first mentioned by a man named Horace Walpole in 1754."

"You've got to be kidding," said one of the other husbands. "You're not telling me you read books from the 1700s!"

Clayton laughed. "No, but I heard it on the radio. Walpole had been reading a fairy tale called *The Three Princes of Serendip*. These three princes would accidentally make fun and exciting discoveries on their way to do something else. He called that serendipity. That's what I like to do on vacation. In fact, I like to do that when I'm not on vacation. I heard someone say that serendipity is putting a quarter in a gumball machine and having three pieces come rattling out instead of one—and all red. I'm looking for all the red gumballs I can find in life."

Hannah just shook her head back and forth. She had heard that story more than once.

As the barbecue discussion progressed, I watched Clayton continue to laugh and talk loudly and rapidly. He was full of high energy and frequently used hand and arm gestures to emphasize his points.

Hannah, on the other hand, had ceased listening to Clayton. She was deep in conversation with one of the other wives. She was not as outgoing or as outspoken as her husband, who was becoming the life of the party.

Hannah was reserved in her responses and felt more comfortable in one-on-one interactions.

Hannah enjoyed talking about politics and what was happening in Washington. She had strong opinions about corruption in the financial markets and on Wall Street. In fact, she carefully researched the backgrounds of the politicians she voted for.

When it came to politics, Clayton, on the other hand, told a lot of jokes.

"My eight-year-old and I were discussing holidays, and I asked him, 'What holiday comes after Halloween and almost always features a turkey?'

"He quickly answered, 'Election day!'"

If that joke brought the proper response, Clayton would follow it up with a half dozen more jokes. He never seemed to take discussions about politics or religion seriously the way Hannah did. She was often very intense.

> The world is governed more by appearances
> than by realities, so that it is fully as necessary
> to seem to know something as to know it.
> —Daniel Webster

Clayton was a risk taker, but Hannah was careful and meticulous.

Clayton spoke before he thought. He often put his foot in his mouth and had to whistle between his toes. Hannah was more serious and controlled in sharing her thoughts, especially in a group setting.

Clayton disliked rules and regulations, but Hannah liked structure and security. Clayton was carefree and enjoyed freedom, but Hannah thrived on accuracy and everything being in its place.

When something went wrong, Clayton blustered and complained like Donald Duck. When things didn't go right for Hannah, she became critical and sarcastic, like the wicked witch in *The Wizard of Oz*.

Clayton's social style was clearly the exact opposite of Hannah's. He was definitely Expressive, and Hannah was very Analytical. But their attraction to each other had nothing to do with their negative habits or qualities. They were captivated by their positive strengths.

Clayton's outgoing and charismatic social style balanced Hannah's quiet, shy, and hesitant social style. Her structure, perfectionism, and follow-through balanced his disorganization and procrastination.

Clayton's unpredictability and spontaneity added excitement to Hannah's routine day. Hannah's stability tempered Clayton's impulsiveness and forcefulness. They were living proof that opposites attract. They also dispelled the gender myth that men are thinkers and women are feelers. Clayton bases most of his decisions on his gut feeling and is very opinionated. He wears his heart on his sleeve and doesn't mind telling people what he feels about things. He doesn't always think through his decisions or analyze things. In fact, he gets annoyed when people spend too much time considering too many details. He would rather just make a decision! When he goes to the polls, he votes according to his feelings about the candidates. He considers himself pretty intuitive and doesn't need to pore over pages of facts and data.

Minds are like parachutes; they work best when open.

—Lord Thomas Dewar

Conversely, Hannah is more of a thinker than a feeler. She enjoys spending a lot of time gathering facts and information before making a decision. She prides herself in not making emotional or irrational decisions and thinks Clayton could really improve in this area. She laughs at the stereotype that men think with their heads and women with their hearts. She knows Clayton is all heart and she is all head. She also recognizes that they both need to learn to be more like the other. Clayton needs to evaluate his decisions more carefully and gather more facts, and Hannah needs to learn how to make decisions without having to gather every possible piece of information she can think of.

Examining Your Own Stereotypes

Take a moment to examine your own beliefs and the stereotypes you may be embracing. Do you think men are better thinkers and women are better feelers? Are you communicating stereotypes to your children or impressionable people around you?

Stereotypes like these can damage relationships and cause people to fall short of their potential in life. If men are convinced they are incapable of deep feeling and emotion, they may never stretch themselves in these areas, and this can stifle their relationships. Additionally, some men may consider themselves ill-suited for some jobs or careers if they have been convinced that certain jobs require more feeling than thinking and are better left to women.

Women who assume that they are not biologically designed to handle high levels of thinking may forego careers that demand analytical skills. Additionally, they may bring these gender stereotypes into personal and professional relationships and misunderstand the people they relate to.

Our society needs a paradigm change regarding gender stereotypes. Looking through a lens of social style instead of gender will shift the focus away from stereotypes and force us to educate ourselves more about social style differences. As you do this, you will notice that many of the differences you have attempted to attribute to gender are really attributable to social style.

For Your Improvement

Reflect on the following questions and write down your answers. Refer back to them as you work toward the improvement of your personal and professional relationships.

1. Do you tend to base your decisions on your feelings or on an analytical thought process?

2. How does this affect your relationships with the people you live and work with?

3. Are you butting heads with anyone who operates differently from you in this area?

4. What else have you learned from this chapter, and how could you effectively apply this information to your personal and professional life?

10

Men Are Decisive,
Women Can't Make Up Their Minds

I *don't know if I can sit through another one of those boring sessions,* Jessica said to herself.

That Tyler Reynolds is such a dork when it comes to leading meetings. No one ever makes any decisions or does anything about the problem.

Both Jessica and Tyler were serving on their Neighborhood Watch committee. It had been formed as a result of a number of recent nearby burglaries and muggings.

Tyler Reynolds was a very likeable and diplomatic fellow. That's why most of the neighbors had insisted he become the leader of the committee. He was the type of person who didn't ruffle people's feathers. Tyler, however, was reluctant to take the position. He suggested several other people's names to get the focus off of himself. He just wanted to quietly attend the meetings and see what the other people in the neighborhood were going to do.

> If a man will begin with certainties, he shall
> end in doubts; but if he will be content to begin
> with doubts he shall end in certainties.
> —Francis Bacon

Jessica was just the opposite. She didn't join the committee to see what other people thought. She joined because she was angry and wanted to stop the burglaries and bring the muggers to justice. She wanted action, not talk.

Jessica was at her desk at work, thinking about the Neighborhood Watch meeting that evening. *If that Tyler Reynolds says, "We can't make any decisions without getting all the facts" one more time, I think I'll scream. Doesn't he know that waiting until you get all the facts leads to a conclusion and not a decision?*

On the other side of town, Tyler was having his own struggle. His stomach was already in knots as he thought about the Neighborhood Watch meeting that evening. He was trying to think of a way to get out of going. The last two meetings had not been fun. They had ended with some raised voices and personal verbal attacks. The most vocal individual was Jessica MacDonald. She had come on very strong. If Tyler hated anything, it was conflict. He would do anything he could to avoid it.

> The percentage of mistakes in quick decisions is no greater than in long, drawn-out vacillations, and the effect of decisiveness itself "makes things go" and creates confidence.
> —Anne O'Hare McCormick

As Tyler thought about the meeting, he remembered what his mother often said: "The test of good manners is being able to put up with bad ones."

Even though he contemplated his mother's words, they didn't seem to help. He wanted to avoid facing Jessica's strong personality. She tended to dominate the discussions and intimidate the people in the group. Then he remembered his father's thoughts about conflict. "I learned a long time ago to never wrestle a pig. You'll get dirty, and besides that, the pig likes it."

That thought caused Tyler to smile inside for a moment. He knew he could never say anything like that even though he felt like it. He then resigned himself to acting like Mahatma Gandhi with nonviolence and tolerance. Tyler let out a sigh.

Making decisions for Tyler was difficult because of his three major fears. The first was his *fear of the unknown.* What would happen if he began to exercise a more decisive leadership style? He was already feeling a little helpless and insecure. His social style didn't allow him to feel comfortable coming on strong. He didn't want people to think he was being pushy.

This fear merged with his *fear of failure.* He didn't want to fail in front of others. Tyler knew that the number one fear in the United States is the fear of public speaking. People want to be in control. They don't want to be seen as incompetent or foolish. He didn't want to make the wrong decision or face the unpleasant task of telling other people he was wrong.

Those two fears combined with Tyler's *fear of rejection*. He wanted to be liked and accepted. He didn't want to be talked about or criticized. He remembered the little poem from his school days: "Sticks and stones may break my bones, but words will never hurt me." He knew that was a lie. Words and comments do hurt.

Jessica was also continuing to struggle with what had gone on in previous meetings. She knew that she needed to control her words. She had strong opinions about everything. However, she was beginning to realize that she didn't need to share everything she was thinking.

Jessica was a bottom-line person who didn't like to listen to long-drawn-out explanations or useless facts and trivia. She liked to get right to the point. She could easily make sound decisions with few facts. And she was usually right. However, she was beginning to see that her social style tended to dominate and overpower other people. She could tell that some in the group were beginning to back away from her and her thoughts.

The whole world steps aside for the man
who knows where he is going.
—anonymous

Jessica was not afraid of conflict and was well-equipped to deal with controversy, but she was having second thoughts. *I may be right about what we need to do,* she thought to herself, *but the way I'm saying it is turning people off.* She reached into her desk and pulled out a three-by-five card with a quote from Abraham Lincoln on it:

> No man resolved to make the most of himself can spare time for personal contention. Still less can he afford to take all the consequences, including the vitiating of his temper, and the loss of self-control. Yield larger things to which you can show no more than equal right; and yield lesser ones, though clearly your own. Better give your path to a dog than be bitten by him in contesting for the right. Even killing the dog would not cure the bite.

Jessica made a commitment to herself. She was going to try to encourage

Tyler to make the important decisions that needed to be made without shoving her timeline down his throat. She was painfully aware that patience was not her virtue, and this was an opportunity to work on that.

By the time the meeting ended, Tyler had stretched himself to make a few key decisions, and Jessica had backed off her aggressive stance. The mood of the meeting was much more cohesive, and everyone left feeling hopeful that they were improving the safety of the neighborhood.

Dispelling the Stereotype

The stereotype tells us that men are decisive and women can't seem to make up their minds. As a result, men take more risks and make better managers and leaders. Additionally, because men are more decisive, they hate shopping with women because women take forever to decide what they want. Conversely, men can get in, make a decision, get what they need, and get out. These are all inaccurate assumptions, myths, and stereotypes.

The way you approach decision making has nothing to do with your gender. It has everything to do with your social style. Take a look at the four different social styles' approach to decision making.

Indecision is like a stepchild: If he does not wash his hands, he is called dirty, if he does, he is wasting water.

—African proverb

How the Four Social Styles Make Decisions

You have an innate instinct about making decisions. That doesn't mean you can't learn to make decisions faster or be more methodical in your approach. It simply means you are predisposed to approaching decisions either quickly or slowly.

Analyticals. These folks tend to be the slowest decision makers. They would rather make no decision than a bad decision. They want to gather all of the facts and data available before making a decision. They love graphs, charts, consumer reports, and detailed information. They want to think about things.

Analyticals are nightmare prospects for time-share salespeople. Time-shares are usually sold on the spot. Analyticals tend to sit on big decisions for at least 24 hours. The two don't mix. An Analytical would rather walk away from the best deal in the world than be pressured into making a decision.

The priorities of an Analytical when approaching decisions are to save face and save money. They see their reputations riding on their decisions, and they don't want to be embarrassed by the decisions they make. So saving face is important to an Analytical. Additionally, they are financially frugal, and they want to be sure they are getting the best value for their money. They are big proponents of quality products and quality decisions. Whether male or female, Analyticals will often make good decisions, but they will make them slowly.

Whenever I make a bum decision, I go
out and make another decision.
—Harry S. Truman

Drivers. Drivers approach decisions with speed and intensity. They would rather make a bad decision than no decision. They just want the decision to be made! They hate graphs, charts, and detailed information.

They can be either dream prospects or nightmare prospects for the time-share salesperson. They will assimilate the information quickly and make a decision. This can be a dream if they decide to buy. It can be a nightmare if they have already made up their mind not to. Giving them more facts and information won't usually sway them. Once their mind is made up, they are adamant about their decisions.

Drivers' priority when making decisions is to save time. They don't want to waste time analyzing a decision too much. They would rather put the decision in motion and adapt to the consequences as they arise. As a result, they don't always focus on the details of the decisions or contingency plans. If you want to get to the moon, hire a Driver. But if you want to get back, hire an Analytical! Analyticals (male and female) pay attention to detail and engage in contingency planning.

Drivers tend to plow through decisions, often appearing to roll over people. If they are in a group and they see that a decision needs to be made, they tend to step up first and lead the group to make a decision.

Amiables. Amiables are similar to Analyticals in their approach to decisions. They would rather make no decision than a bad decision. The major difference is their priority. Amiables' priority is to save relationships, so they want to carefully evaluate how their decisions will affect others and be perceived by others. They want people to like them, and they don't want to make waves. If Amiables perceive that their decisions will cause conflict, they will often avoid making those decisions at all.

Amiables will sometimes get pushed into making decisions they don't want to make, because they want to spare someone's feelings (like a time-share salesperson). They find it difficult to say no to people. To avoid the conflict that sometimes comes with saying no, they may avoid people or circumstances. In groups, they will often wait for others to speak up before making decisions. If the majority of the group is leaning one direction, the Amiable will likely follow to be agreeable. Whether male or female, Amiables tend to go with the flow on decisions and avoid controversies if at all possible.

Expressives. Expressives, like Drivers, make decisions quickly but for different reasons. Drivers tend to be more rational and unemotional about their decisions. Expressives tend to be more intuitive and base decisions on gut feelings. Their emotions will play a large role in the way they make decisions. For example, if Expressives are in a time-share presentation, a large part of their decision will depend on the way they feel about the salesperson and whether they connect.

We can try to avoid making choices by doing
nothing, but even that is a decision.
—Gary Collins

Expressives' top priority is to save energy. Looking at charts, graphs, and detailed information takes too much energy for Expressives. They are social people, and if something isn't fun and doesn't involve socializing, they want to avoid it. They are often impatient and expect others to make decisions quickly as well. Expressives are often accused of making rash decisions or not thinking before they act. Like Drivers, Expressives would rather make bad decisions than no decision. Whether male or female, Expressives make decisions.

Shopping for Stereotypes

Back to Josh and Bri. Josh is an Expressive, and Bri is an Analytical.

The gender myth states that women like to shop and men don't. If you take Josh shopping to a place that has things he likes and he is able to shop and make decisions at his own pace, he's happy. If you put him in the shower curtain section at Wal-Mart with Bri while she analyzes her many choices, he's miserable.

"It's a stupid shower curtain, for crying out loud! Make a decision already!" He doesn't pretend to be patient.

"Josh, I want to look at what's available, what matches our bathroom, and compare prices. You're welcome to go browse the latest paintball guns if this bores you." He didn't have to be told twice. Bri could smell the rubber from his shoes burning from the friction against the floor as he raced down the store aisle.

An observer might assume that Bri is a typical woman and Josh is a typical man. This assumption would be the result of strongly reinforced stereotypes. Josh is very decisive, and Bri can be indecisive. These approaches to their decision-making processes are not the result of gender, but of social style.

Making Decisions and Taking Risks

Another stereotype often accompanies the one about decisiveness. Supposedly, because men are more decisive, they take bigger risks. This plays out in finance, relationships, and extreme sports. Conversely, women allegedly seek stability, tranquility, and safety.

As with decision making, your tendency toward risk taking follows your social style, not your gender. Additionally, your likeliness to take risks is directly related to your approach to decision making.

Drivers and Expressives are quick to make decisions. They are also the risk takers. They are much more willing and likely to take risks than Amiables or Analyticals, who prefer safety and stability, whether male or female.

Decisiveness and Leadership

The book *Culture, Leadership, and Organizations: The GLOBE Study of 62 Societies* is about a survey of 17,000 people in 62 different countries. It identifies 22 universally desirable leadership traits. One of those traits was decisiveness. Followers want leaders who can make decisions.

If society categorized this trait as a predominately male trait, couldn't we conclude that many women are ill-equipped to be effective leaders?

Additionally, assertiveness and risk-taking ability are also considered necessary for effective leadership. These have been considered masculine traits because of long-lasting stereotypes. Other necessary leadership traits and behaviors include giving credit to others and being collaborative, which tend to be viewed as more feminine traits—additional inaccurate stereotyping.

Decision: Something a man makes when he
cannot get anyone to serve on a committee.
—Fletcher Knebel

A complete list of every trait that is necessary for effective leadership would include traits from all four social styles. This means that people who would be effective leaders (whether male or female) must learn to demonstrate behaviors of each social style. Some of these behaviors may come naturally, and some may require concentration and practice.

Decisiveness is a necessary trait for leaders, and it will come naturally for Drivers and Expressives. Amiables and Analyticals will have to work on this area. On the other hand, patience is also necessary for effective leadership. Drivers and Expressives usually stink in this area, but it comes naturally to Amiables and Analyticals. Gender is irrelevant when it comes to this issue—social style is what determines natural tendencies.

Once you make a decision, the universe
conspires to make it happen.
—Ralph Waldo Emerson

Survey Says

In my survey, I asked respondents which statement fits more: "I make thoughtful decisions" or "I make quick decisions." More men than women indicated a tendency toward quick decisions. If I left the research at that (as many experts do), I would be able to reaffirm the stereotype that men are more decisive than women. However, factoring in social style changes the meaning of the results.

When we dig deeper and cross-reference gender responses to social style, the results make sense. We would expect Drivers and Expressives to make quick decisions, and we would expect Amiables and Analyticals to make thoughtful decisions.

The 128 males who responded to the survey included 67 Drivers and 61 Expressives. The 109 females who responded included 54 Drivers and 55 Expressives. More male Drivers and Expressives responded than female Drivers and Expressives, so naturally, more men than women indicated a tendency toward quick decisions. The results reflect social style, not gender.

Much of the research on gender issues presupposes gender differences. When studies show differences between the genders, researchers simply assume that the differences are based on gender. Social style is never taken into consideration. This is why so many of the studies and their results conflict with each other. If researchers cross-referenced their gender studies with social-style analysis, the results would most likely align with the discussions in this book.

Analytical	Driver
indecisive	decisive
no decision better than a bad decision	bad decision better than no decision
priority: save face and money	priority: save time
Amiable	**Expressive**
indecisive	decisive
no decision better than a bad decision	bad decision better than no decision
priority: save relationships	priority: save energy

Fig. 10A. Social styles and decision making.

For Your Improvement

Reflect on the following questions and write down your answers. Refer back to them as you work toward the improvement of your personal and professional relationships.

1. Do you tend to be decisive or indecisive?

2. How does this affect your relationships with the people you live and work with?

3. What steps can you take to achieve balance between being overly analytical and being rash?

4. What else have you learned from this chapter, and how could you effectively apply this information to your personal and professional life?

Part 2:

Overcoming Gender Lies with the Truth About Social Style

11

Other Gender Myths

This chapter includes more gender myths that are floating around society. As you look at these stereotypes, consider which ones you have bought into. As you will discover in the next chapter, the power and influence of stereotypes affects your life and relationships even if you are not aware of it. See if any of these gender myths look familiar to you.

The myth: Women use language to send and receive emotional signals; men use language to send and receive information.

The truth: The tendency to use language a certain way has nothing to do with gender. It has more to do with social style. Analyticals and Drivers tend to focus on facts and information, but Amiables and Expressives tend to focus on the emotional element in communication.

The myth: Women tend to take everything personally; men tend to take everything impersonally.

The truth: Individuals who lean toward the Analytical or Amiable social style tend to receive input personally. On the other hand, Drivers and Expressives tend to take comments and situations more impersonally.

The myth: Women like to go shopping; men get in, get what they need, and get out.

The truth: Drivers hate to shop regardless of their gender. They get in, get what they need, and get out. Analyticals like to compare prices at different places. Amiables go with the flow on shopping, and Expressives like the social interaction of being out in public in general.

The myth: Women are more interested in nitty-gritty details; men are interested in general principles, abstract ideas, and philosophy.

The truth: Analyticals and Amiables are more interested in details, facts, and how things interrelate. Drivers and Expressives (men and women) have little interest in a multitude of details. They want to know the goal, the principle, and the bottom line. They are big-picture people.

The myth: A woman's home is an extension of her personality; a man's job is an extension of his personality.

The truth: This concept may have an element of truth in it because many women do not work outside the home. However, a home is an extension of many men's personalities, and a job is also an extension of many working women's personalities. Personality is displayed at home and at work by both men and women according to their own social style.

The myth: Women tend to become involved in activities more easily and quickly; men tend to stand back, evaluate, and volunteer slowly.

The truth: Shyness and disinterest are not gender issues. Analyticals and Amiables tend to be a little withdrawn, and Drivers and Expressives are generally more outgoing. On the other hand, Analyticals and Drivers lean toward accomplishing tasks, and Amiables and Expressives lean toward nurturing relationships rather than launching into activity.

The myth: Women like security, men like risk.

The truth: Risk taking and the need for security are not gender issues. Analyticals and Amiables tend to desire stability and financial security. Drivers and Expressives are willing to take more risks, hoping for the bigger return. Even in nonfinancial situations, Drivers and Expressives tend to take more risks than Amiables and Analyticals.

The myth: Women like cats and small, cuddly animals; men like dogs and big, burly animals.

The truth: Plenty of women hate cats, and plenty of men own teacup poodles. Drivers do not generally gravitate toward small, cuddly animals. Drivers are not the most warm and fuzzy people in the world, so you won't hear them say, "Awww…" when someone shoves a kitten in their face.

The myth: Women tend to become depressed under stress or in conflict; men tend to explode under stress or in conflict.

The truth: Your natural response to conflict is not dictated by your gender. It is determined by your social style and what you were taught growing up. Your first, instinctual response to conflict is to give in if you're an Amiable, attack or explode if you're an Expressive, withdraw if you're an Analytical, and control if you're a Driver. Amiables and Analyticals get more depressed about stress and conflict than Drivers and Expressives do.

The myth: Women are cooperative, men are competitive.

The truth: Women can be just as competitive as men. This too is a social-style issue, not a gender issue. Drivers and Expressives tend to be more competitive than Amiables and Analyticals. Drivers are especially competitive, regardless of gender. If you're not convinced women can be competitive, take a look at Hilary Clinton (a Driver) in the 2008 presidential primary race.

The myth: Women are always late; men are always on time (waiting for women).

The truth: You will see this myth perpetuated in movies and sitcoms. Men are always waiting on women, who habitually run late. But it's not a gender issue. Drivers and Analyticals are rarely ever late. They are usually on time and are often early. Amiables and Expressives tend to run late unless they have a Driver or Analytical secondary element to their social style.

The myth: Women never forget, men never remember.

The truth: You have probably met plenty of ditzy women. They have been fodder for all the blonde jokes. And some men are walking encyclopedias. Gender is not the issue. Analyticals can be very legalistic, Drivers can be revengeful, Amiables can be procrastinators, and Expressives can be extremely forgetful.

The myth: Women want to just talk through problems or be listened to; men want to take control and solve problems.

The truth: Your approach to problems is a social-style issue, not a gender issue. Drivers want to take the bull by the horns and control and solve the problem quickly. Analyticals want to analyze and think through it. Amiables want to collaborate with others first. Expressives want to talk and vent about the problem, and they want to give everyone else unsolicited advice on how to solve their problems.

The myth: Women are tactful, men are blunt.

The truth: Amiables and Analyticals tend to be more tactful and gracious because they hate conflict. Drivers and Expressives tend to be blunt and to the point, often offending people with their approach. This is definitely not a gender issue. You have probably met some abrasive women and some diplomatic men.

The myth: Women are bad drivers; men are good drivers.

The truth: You have probably encountered plenty of terrible drivers, whether men or women. This too is not a gender issue. Amiables and Analyticals tend to drive slower and more carefully. Expressives and Drivers tend to take more risks, drive faster, and be less patient.

The myth: Women take on guilt; men take on resentment.

The truth: There are plenty of resentful women and guilt-prone men in this world. Drivers and Expressives seem to struggle more with anger issues (resentfulness) and Analyticals and Amiables with fear issues (guilt). This is a universal human-nature problem, not a gender issue.

The myth: Women are like computers—their minds keep going until a problem is solved. Men are like filing cabinets that store problems—they can close the drawer and forget the problem.

The truth: This has nothing to do with gender. Analyticals and Amiables tend to replay information and situations over and over again in their thinking. Drivers and Expressives (men and women) are interested in new developments and future situations and tend to leave the past behind.

Let's close this chapter with a humorous look at some actual gender differences. Whether these are based on social acceptance or really do have to do with gender is yet to be determined. Regardless, you will never see most men do any of the things listed below.

The Top Five Things You Will Never See a Man Do

5. pass toilet paper under the stall in a public restroom

4. borrow his friend's jeans

3. ask his buddy to go to the bathroom with him

2. try on his friend's clothes

1. talk to the person in the stall next to him in a public bathroom

---

If a woman has to choose between catching
a fly ball and saving an infant's life, she will
choose to save the infant's life without even
considering whether there are men on base.

—Dave Barry

For Your Improvement

Reflect on the following questions and write down your answers. Refer back to them as you work toward the improvement of your personal and professional relationships.

1. What gender myths have you bought into?

2. How can you start to make changes in your perceptions and beliefs regarding gender?

3. What else have you learned from this chapter, and how could you effectively apply this information to your personal and professional life?

12

The Power and Influence
of Stereotypes

Ryan sat at his desk in his room, wondering why he felt so lost. He had one year left of high school, and his parents and teachers were pressuring him to make some decisions about his future. What did he want to study in college? What kind of job did he want to ultimately hold? What were his goals in life? He was terrified of letting people down, especially his father.

Ryan's dad was a Driver: goal-oriented, ambitious, tenacious, tough, and successful. He owned a law firm and was a prominent member of the community. Ryan was his only child, and he just wanted the best for his son. Ryan's mom was a soft-spoken Amiable who tried to compensate for the somewhat militant demeanor of Ryan's father. She often coddled Ryan and let things slide through the years, hoping to provide some balance to his demanding father.

> Instead of being presented with stereotypes by age, sex, color, class, or religion, children must have the opportunity to learn that within each range, some people are loathsome and some are delightful.
> —Margaret Mead

Ryan inherited most of his mom's social style and was much more laid-back and easygoing than his father. He was eager to please both of his parents, but he generally felt an unconditional acceptance from his mom. Though he was six feet two, he felt dwarfed by his father's success and drive.

He knew his father loved him, but he often questioned whether his father thought he was a man's man.

His dad had played football in high school and college and was extremely competitive. Ryan didn't care much for sports and felt the sting of his father's disapproval when he gravitated toward music instead.

Ryan wasn't much of a risk-taker either. His father spent much of Ryan's childhood trying to get him to engage in riskier activities than Ryan was comfortable with. When Ryan was six, his father hung a tire swing in the yard. He put Ryan in the swing and gave him a slight push. Ryan hated the feeling in his stomach and pleaded to stop. His father eased him off the swing and lowered him to the ground. Even at the age of six, Ryan could sense his father's disappointment. When Ryan was ten, his father took him ATV riding and tried to get Ryan to take some riskier trails. When Ryan began to cry, his father scolded him for being a sissy and reminded him as he had so many times before that boys don't cry when things get tough— they get tough too! As hard as Ryan tried to fight back the tears, they always seemed to stream down his face in his most vulnerable moments.

When Ryan was fourteen, his first girlfriend broke his heart. He sat in the garage with his head in his hands, weeping and pleading for God to make the pain go away. When his father opened the garage door to grab a tool, Ryan tried to hide his tears. His father asked him what was wrong. Ryan explained that his girlfriend had called off the relationship—and in a note, of all things. His father shook his head and said, "Ryan, if there's one thing you need to learn in life it's this: People will let you down and let you go. There's no use crying over it. The best thing you can do is suck it up, move on, and take it like a man."

Crude classifications and false generalizations
are the curse of organized life.
—George Bernard Shaw

Those were the words he had heard so many times growing up: "Take it like a man." What did that mean exactly? Ryan had never seen his father cry—ever. He was strong, confident, and fearless. He was truly a man's man. So why was Ryan so different? Why did he feel like less of a man every time he cried? Why did he feel like less of a man when he felt afraid?

Ryan's father wondered why Ryan was so different too. Why was he so passive? Why did he let his friends take control in so many situations? Why didn't he stand up for himself more or have stronger opinions on things that were so important? Ryan's father had worked hard to instill what he considered a strong work ethic into his son. He talked about setting goals and having drive and ambition in life. He believed he set an example for his son to follow. He wondered if Ryan was just trying to spite him by doing the opposite of everything he tried to teach him. Why wasn't his son more tough and manly, like he was? Why was he so sensitive? What was he doing wrong as a father? Was it because Ryan's mother was too soft on him?

Ryan had some tough decisions to make. His father always wanted him to become a lawyer. Ryan wanted to please his dad, so he had tried to show an interest in his dad's law firm and had begun to study law early in high school. It didn't take long for Ryan to realize it just didn't fit him. First of all, he hated to argue with people, and that's all he saw lawyers doing. His own father was a master at arguing and debating, and Ryan admired his abilities. Ryan, however, became tense at the first sign of conflict and tried to keep the peace when any tension arose. The thought of becoming a lawyer terrified him.

Ryan wanted to work with children and possibly become a teacher. He wanted to be around people and help others as much as he could. But would his father think less of him? It just didn't seem like the manly way to go. His father always commented about how women made such great teachers because they had the compassion, patience and kindness for it. Besides, women were much more nurturing, so teaching was a natural fit for them.

Ryan sat staring at his desk, wondering how he could possibly broach the subject with his father. How could he make him understand that he felt compassion and nurturing toward kids and really wanted to be a teacher? How could he explain to his father that he was so much different inside and didn't understand why? Ryan couldn't help feeling weak, alone, and afraid.

Misunderstanding Runs Deep

The power of stereotypes extends into the deepest areas of our lives, areas we don't always want to talk about. We program ourselves and others with all sorts of stereotypes that affect the way we think and act in our daily lives. We are told from a very young age what is normal for girls and what is normal for boys. We attempt to mold our children into these stereotypes and find ourselves disconnected from them when they don't comply.

Ryan's father wanted Ryan to be like him—a Driver. His father associated all the traits of a Driver with being masculine. Traits like assertiveness, ambition, drive, toughness, risk taking, fearlessness, confidence, competence, and a task orientation. Ryan turned out to be more Amiable, taking after his mother. Some of the common traits of an Amiable are associated with being feminine: compassion, caring, nurturing, compliance, cooperativeness, emotional sensitivity, and fear.

Ryan's father most likely grew up with gender stereotypes that reaffirmed his feeling of manliness. His own father probably beamed with pride when he took risks, showed assertiveness, and demonstrated high levels of competitiveness. He probably heard things like, "That's my boy," "Boys will be boys," and "He's all boy!"

> If we all worked on the assumption that
> what is accepted as true were really true,
> there would be little hope of advance.
>
> —Orville Wright

Ryan spent most of his childhood trying to hide his feelings, choke back his emotions, and "be a man." He didn't like being teased by the kids at school for being too sensitive, so he tried to suppress his emotions as much as he could. The older he got, the better he became at it.

The failure to understand social style in yourself and others can lead to deep feelings of confusion and frustration about yourself and your loved ones. When we place stereotypical judgments on people and expect them to adhere to behaviors we consider normal and within the boundaries of our gender stereotypes, we create more conflict. The power and influence of these stereotypes can affect people for a lifetime and cause them to question their identity and self-worth.

It's Not Just Gender

Stereotypes of any kind carry a great amount of power and influence. We tend to live up or down to the projections that are placed upon us. If we are continually told we will do poorly in a particular area because of gender, race, income level, demographic location, and the like, we often comply.

Stereotypes become ingrained in us whether we realize it or not. They become ingrained through our parents, off-the-cuff comments, media stories, racial jokes, and so on. You may think that these things don't affect you, that you don't allow stereotypes to alter the way you view certain people or make decisions, but they do.

Try this exercise. Log on to www.Implicit.Harvard.edu and fill out an IAT (Implicit Association Test). When the home page loads, click on the button that says *Demonstration*. From there you can select the featured task or other demonstrations. The purpose of the exercise is to show you how you may very well be biased about certain issues based on the stereotypes you have been fed.

The first test I took was a race test. I was asked at the beginning of the test a series of questions to establish if I preferred white people to black. Of course I answered that I viewed both races equally, because I do.

I was then asked to put my right index finger on the letter *I* and my left index finger on the letter *E*. Pictures and words flashed up on the screen in different blocks. The pictures were of black people and white people. The words were positive words (like *love, friend, laughter,* and *peace*) and negative words (like *hurt, agony, failure,* and *evil*).

In one block, I was instructed to rapidly click on the letter *I* whenever a picture of a white person or a positive word appeared on the screen. I was asked to click the letter *E* whenever a black person or a negative word appeared on the screen. Then the words were reversed so I was asked to click on the letter *I* whenever a black person or a positive word appeared and the letter *E* whenever a white person or a negative word appeared. I was asked to perform the exercise as quickly as possible to reveal my instinctual responses.

Many people find it more difficult to rapidly associate black people with positive words. Some experts attribute this phenomenon to the many news stories and media coverage associating black people to crimes. Others attribute it to the deeply held prejudices that have existed in our culture and society.

I deplore racism and consider myself an objective person. I was shocked and appalled at the completion of the test when the computer screen told me that I moderately preferred white people to black. I was sure there must be some other explanation as to why it was harder for me to quickly select positive words coupled with black faces. The test bothered me, so I took another one. This time, I took the gender/science test.

The concept was similar except there were no pictures, only words. One set of word choices were male (like *dad, uncle, grandpa, boy,* and *man*) or female (like *mother, sister, aunt, girl,* and *woman*). Another set of word choices dealt with science (like *biology, physics, chemistry, math,* and *engineering*) versus liberal arts (like *philosophy, humanities, arts, literature,* and *music*).

The test proceeded to have me associate liberal arts words with women and science words with men. I was then asked to associate science words with women and liberal arts words with men. Again, the objective was to make my selections as quickly as possible to reveal an unconscious bias I may have.

Many people think they are thinking when they
are merely rearranging their prejudices.
—William James

As I started the test, I thought it would surely show my impartiality. Considering the title of the book here, I would consider myself to be relatively free of gender biases. As I completed the test, I was disappointed to see that I had a moderate association of men to science and women to liberal arts. This seems to reveal attitudes that have been imprinted on my mind that I was not even aware of.

The IAT reveals our strongly held stereotypes through the way we associate words and pictures with different groups of people. I encourage you to go to the website and take some of the tests they offer there. The choices include religion, skin tone, race, age, and disability. These tests will give you a better understanding of strongly held stereotypes that might be affecting your associations.

Expectations Created by Stereotypes

Gender stereotypes create similar positive and negative expectations of performance and behavior. For example, the IAT highlights the common gender stereotype that men are good at math and science and women are good at liberal arts. Studies have shown that these gender stereotypes create self-fulfilling prophecies. People tend to perform according to the stereotypes they have believed. So when boys are reminded that girls are bad at math and they are good at math, they do better at math. And of course it is no surprise that when girls are reminded of the stereotype, their performance in math drops.

Stubbornness we deprecate, firmness we condone. The former is our neighbor's trait, the latter is our own.
—John Wooden

Bringing stereotypes to the forefront of people's minds reinforces the self-stereotype. American women have been stereotyped as not being good at math. But Asians have been stereotyped as being great at math. So how do Asian-American women view themselves with regard to math? The answer depends on which stereotype is brought to the forefront of their minds.

A psychologist for the University of Virginia, Stacey Sinclair, conducted a study in 2006 to answer this question. Sinclair addressed the gender stereotypes that Western women are good at verbal skills and bad at math but Asians are good at math.

So she asked 62 Asian-American women to rate themselves on how well they would do in tests regarding verbal skills or tests that deal with math. They were also asked to rate how they felt others (like teachers) would rate them in these key areas. Half of the group was asked to identify their ethnicity at the top of the page and half were asked to identify their gender.

The group that was asked to identify their gender had the stereotype brought to the forefront of their mind that women are good at verbal skills but bad at math. These women rated themselves as better at verbal skills and said others would rate them that way as well.

The group that was asked to identify their ethnicity were reminded of the stereotype that Asians are better at math. These women rated their math abilities more favorably than their verbal skills and said that others would rate them the same. The power and influence of stereotypes is astounding. It would appear that the more prominent and well-known the stereotype, the deeper the effect on the individual.

The greatest friend of truth is time, her greatest enemy is prejudice, and her constant companion is humility.
—Charles Caleb Colton

The Effects of Nullifying Stereotypes

Three researchers (V.K. Gupta, D.B. Turban, and N.M. Bhawe) conducted a 2008 study to examine the impact of gender stereotypes on men's and women's intentions to pursue entrepreneurship. Stereotypically masculine traits have traditionally been attributed to entrepreneurs: assertiveness, aggressiveness, risk taking, extroversion, task orientation, and the like.

In this study, researchers tested the entrepreneurial intention of both males and females when presented with implicit (subtle), explicit (blatant), and gender-neutral (nullified) stereotypes. When the stereotype was nullified, men and women showed a fairly equal result toward entrepreneurial intention.

Many researchers suggest that educators avoid using typically male words to describe entrepreneurs or any other field that is often related to male traits like aggressiveness and assertiveness. Researchers have made this recommendation for many years. But it's not working, for good reason.

The words themselves have been linked with masculine characteristics, just as words like *compassionate* and *sympathetic* have been attributed to female characteristics. So researchers suggest using gender-neutral words to describe jobs, tasks, and careers.

It is time for parents to teach young people early on that in diversity there is beauty and there is strength.

—Maya Angelou

This creates a problem because some jobs and careers do require assertiveness or risk taking and should be described as such. We need to educate educators so they can educate others that these words do not define masculine or feminine—they define social style. Educators themselves must understand that some women can possess just as must assertiveness as some men and some men can possess just as must compassion as some women.

Once this revelation takes place, researchers can begin to adopt a different paradigm about gender stereotypes, and educators can begin to pass on this important information, starting at very young ages.

Begin the Process of Change in the Home

If you are a parent, you can do a lot to free your children from the stereotypes that plague kids every day and cause them to take these stereotypes into adulthood. The first step is to educate yourself. With a stronger understanding of social style, you will be less likely to project the gender stereotypes you were taught onto the next generation. Also, an understanding of social styles will help you understand why your children think and act the way they do.

Your child inherited her social style genetically, but she may have received her predominant style from your spouse and not you. This may explain why your child is so different from you and help you accept those differences.

Try to discover and value your child's own social style and convey your appreciation of her uniqueness and differences. This doesn't mean you shouldn't encourage her to improve in the areas of weakness; it just means you won't try to mold her into something she is not. You will never be able to turn an Amiable into a Driver. However, you can encourage your Amiable to take initiative, set goals, and take a stand on issues.

Parents have become so convinced that educators know what is best for their children that they forget that they themselves are really the experts.
—Marian Wright Edelman

As a parent, you can also educate your children regarding their own social styles. You can let your Driver child know that he will struggle with impatience and always wanting to be in control. You can talk about some constructive ways he can adapt to get along with his friends. You can spend time letting your Analytical child know that people will often see her as antisocial and withdrawn and give her some constructive ways to deal with her own social style as well as her friends'. You can help your Expressive child learn self-discipline so he can sit still and pay attention in class. You can teach him how to control his impulsive nature and cope with the many emotions he feels. By understanding social styles yourself and teaching your kids to understand them, you can begin to make sense of certain behaviors and think of ways to improve.

You can also help your children understand that their friends will be different from them because their friends will also have different social styles. An Analytical child may not be able to understand or relate to an Expressive very well. As parents intervene with positive and constructive ways to deal with different social styles, children will begin to learn how to interact with others and build positive relationships at a young age.

You don't have to wait for teachers to show your children how to solve conflicts and build cohesive relationships. In fact, that training must come from you, and it should start when your children are very young. It takes an investment of time and energy, but the rewards you and your children will reap are enormous. It will be well worth your effort.

For Your Improvement

Reflect on the following questions and write down your answers. Refer back to them as you work toward the improvement of your personal and professional relationships.

1. How have stereotypes influenced your life?

2. How have you stereotyped the people around you?

3. What else have you learned from this chapter, and how could you effectively apply this information to your personal and professional life?

13

Determining Social Style Mind-Set

Communication is like a doubled-edged sword—it can either bring healing or harm to relationships. We will be much more likely to bring healing if we understand how people are wired. Regardless of their gender, people's personalities are based on four basic social style responses that go a long way to determine the way they communicate with family members, friends, coworkers, and even strangers.

> Some people make cutting remarks, but
> the words of the wise bring healing.
> —Proverbs 12:18

Because of these four social styles, people not only view life differently from each other but also communicate in different ways. To effectively get along with people who are similar to us or completely different, we need to understand their frame of reference. We can then modify our behavior and words and enjoy meaningful communication. This will open up lines of understanding and reduce conflict.

The Analytical Mind-Set

Analyticals are self-motivated and determined. They tend to use their energy to increase their technical knowledge, which can become staggering. They can often find cracks or holes in systems and procedures. They tend to do things themselves and focus on completing tasks.

Things Analyticals Like

security	structure	critical thinking
accuracy	facts	organization
stability	competence	logic
quality	details	deductive reasoning
tradition	rules and regulations	

Things Analyticals Don't Like

inaccuracy	evasiveness	clutter
incompetence	mediocrity	disorganization
change	inadequacy	clamor
aggressive people	exaggeration	hastiness
shouting	invasiveness	

The Driver Mind-Set

Drivers are self directed, goal oriented, and persistent. They respond to deadlines and take them seriously. Sometimes they overcommit themselves. They tend to do things themselves and focus on completing tasks.

Things Drivers Like

achievement	control	leadership
challenge	responsibility	independence
success	goals	making decisions
power	debates	productivity
efficiency	competition	

Things Drivers Don't Like

indecisiveness	emotionalism	laziness
boredom	dependency	procrastination
small talk	excuses	taking orders
details	irresponsibility	overanalysis
hypersensitivity	lethargy	

The Amiable Mind-Set

Amiables enjoy developing policies, procedures, and systems that prioritize relationships. They can be devoted to the care of individuals in a group and can enjoy being part of a team. They tend to get things done through other people and focus their efforts on relationships.

Things Amiables Like

contributing	peace and quiet	kindness
loyalty	coaching	comfortable situations
compassion	approval	good relationships
cooperation	cohesiveness	benevolence and concern
friendliness	people they can trust	

Things Amiables Don't Like

conflict	harshness	disharmony
impatience	rushing	yelling
disrespect	pressure	pushiness
discourteousness	tension	rudeness
insensitivity	controversy	

The Expressive Mind-Set

Expressives are outgoing, optimistic, and gregarious. They like action and movement and often focus on short-term goals. They are cheerleaders for those around them. They tend to get things done through other people and focus on relationships.

Things Expressives Like

freedom	vision	creativity
excitement	enthusiasm	innovation
adventure	change	benevolence
flexibility	unpredictability	versatility
spontaneity	uniqueness	

Things Expressives Don't Like

rules	stagnation	lack of creativity
structure	slowness	details
schedules	boredom	formality
routine	ritual	
tedium	unoriginality	

Communicating Effectively with Each Social Style

"Shut up! Shut up! Shut up!" said Mario as he slammed the door and stomped out in anger. This was not the first time he reacted this way. It had become a pattern every time he was confronted with conflict.

If people around you will not hear you, fall
down before them and beg their forgiveness,
for in truth you are to blame.

—Fyodor Dostoyevsky

When Mario was growing up, his family yelled, slammed doors, and even threw things. He never had any models of healthy conflict resolution. He had no chance to develop positive communication skills.

Carla, on the other hand, came from a quiet home. In fact, everyone in her family repressed their ideas and feelings. No one talked about their disagreements. They simply dropped into a world of silence, like a tortoise pulling its head into its shell. Her family members held their hurts, fears, and angers inside. She too had no opportunity to develop effective communication skills.

At home, we learn and establish habits of effective communication or unhealthy communication. But it doesn't stop there. We also develop communication skills through our interaction with friends, schoolmates, coworkers, fellow community members, and even strangers.

We will always be communicating and learning to communicate better, and both can be difficult at times. To begin with, language itself is not precise. For example, consider the word *father*. That word can have different meanings to different people, including these:

| loving father | God our Father | priest |
| mean father | old man | founder |

The sender of a message is more responsible for the message than the hearer is. This is because the speaker knows the meaning of the message and the reason for it. These are not always clear to the person receiving the message.

The speaker is also responsible to communicate emotion. When working on problems, speakers can seem to be attacking individuals rather than attacking issues. Listeners can mistake disagreement with their ideas for personal attacks. Obviously, you may like people but not agree with their ideas or conclusions. This separation is difficult for many people to make.

When talking to others, try to use *I* words and phrases rather than *you* words or phrases. *You* phrases like these can signal an attack:

"You never..."

"You always..."

"Every time you..."

"You can't..."

"You don't..."

David Augsburger, in his book *When Caring Is Not Enough,* lists 20 Dirty Fighting Strategies that people use when trying to get their way. These strategies destroy true communication and cause turmoil in relationships regardless of the social style or gender of the parties.

1. Time: Catch others off guard rather than choose a mutually beneficial time.

2. Turf: Pick your best turf rather than choose a neutral place.

3. Anxiety: Create tension instead of establishing a caring atmosphere.

4. Fog: Filibuster and fume instead of communicating equally.

5. Mystify: Ramble, chain react, and confuse instead of being clear and honest.

6. Generalize: Universalize and exaggerate instead of simplifying and focusing.

7. Analyze: Intellectualize, theorize, and advise instead of admitting pain.

8. Gunnysack: Save up grievances rather than deal with the here and now.

9. Neutrality: Be silent, superior, and detached rather than open and present.

10. Temper: Hide anger and then ventilate rage rather than manage anger effectively.

11. Blame: Find who is at fault rather than practice no-fault fights.

12. Righteousness: Find who is right instead of what is right.

13. Exit: Walk out, clam up, or shut off instead of working things through.

14. Question: Use clever or concealed questions instead of statements.

15. Triangle: Pit people against people instead of dealing with issues firsthand.

16. Put-down: Use sarcasm, jibes, and digs instead of sharing humor.

17. Undermine: Weaken self-esteem rather than enrich self-respect.

18. Guilt: Play either judge or martyr to hook guilt, not responsibility.

19. Mind reading: Read or rape people's minds rather than listen, wait, and learn.

20. Delay: Ignore, forget, or postpone rather than honor commitments.

On the other hand, successful communication begins with the use of *I* words. *I* phrases are more honest, more assertive, and less likely to come across as an attack to the individual.

"I am disappointed…"

"I am angry about…"

"I don't care for…"

"I am hurt over…"

"I would like to see…"

Ideas for Communicating with Analyticals

Provide lots of facts.

Give an organized presentation.

Use logical thinking.

Talk softly and slowly.

Be specific.

Stress the quality of the relationship you would like to have.

Allow time for questions.

Validate their opinions.

Don't exaggerate.

Don't push them to make a decision or share feelings until they are ready.

Don't fight with them or have an extended argument.

Ideas for Communicating with Drivers

Get to the point.

Let them stay in control.

Be confident and businesslike.

Keep your presentation brief and fast-paced.

Ask their opinion.

Don't try to overpower them with words.

Stay away from chitchat and small talk.

Try not to belabor your points.

Don't pressure them—that could escalate the conflict.

Keep on track and off tangents.

Avoid being drawn into an argument.

Ideas for Communicating with Amiables

Show kindness.

Be friendly.

Make them feel valued.

Be patient.

Treat them gently.

Listen to them.

Empathize with their concerns.

Stay relaxed and don't get uptight.

Smile.

Speak softly.

Value their opinions.

Avoid sarcasm.

Try not to rush them.

Ideas for Communicating with Expressives

Socialize and joke around with them.

Be informal.

Make a colorful or vivid presentation.

Talk with excitement.

Ask about their interests and their personal lives.

Keep the conversation fast-paced.

Don't be too serious.

Don't bore them with details.

Don't be stuffy or too concerned about rules.

Don't interrupt them or cut them short.

Talk about how you would like to see the relationship in the future.

Helping Quiet People to Open Up

I'll pay more for a man's ability to express himself than for any other quality he might possess.
—Charles Schwab

As the saying goes, "Still water runs deep." Quiet individuals may outwardly seem to withdraw from interaction, but they actually may be thinking deeply or pondering their thoughts. Still, their silence is sometimes difficult to deal with. Listed below are several communication starters for nonverbal folks. To help them get in touch with their feelings and share their thoughts, suggest that they complete the appropriate sentence.

"I have really been feeling angry about..."

"I feel embarrassed to say..."

"I get very upset when you..."

"This is difficult for me to say, but..."

"Talking about this makes me wonder..."

"I would like you to consider..."

"What bugs me the most is..."

Questions like these can also help quiet folks get started talking:

"I'd love to hear about..."

"I'm interested in hearing more…"

"I'd be happy to listen concerning…"

"How are things with…"

"What do you think about…"

You might also try these "Seven *W*s to Prime the Communication Pump" and bring on a flow of words.

Where did you go?

When did it occur?

Why was the event planned?

Who was there?

What did you talk about?

What did you do?

What was your reaction?

Helping Angry People to Communicate Calmly

Occasionally we will encounter people who are upset or angry. Some issue or circumstance has rubbed them the wrong way, and they are going to tell us about it. Their voices may be raised, and they might attack us with harsh words.

Try to listen carefully and attentively to what they are saying. Endeavor to discover what the main point or real issue is. Try not to take their outbursts personally. Remaining calm and cool is very important. Don't retaliate with your own eruption of anger.

Let them get it all out of their system and express their complete thoughts. When they stop, you might ask them if they would like to share anything else. Be prepared. They may share more hostility.

Try to get a grasp of their problems and restate them. This will indicate that you have been listening to their concerns. Ask them if you have correctly understood their comments.

Ask angry individuals what they would like from you. When you clearly understand what they want, you will mostly be able to choose from these three basic responses:

1. You can say yes with sentences like these: "I can help you out. I can answer your request. I will try and satisfy you."

2. You can compassionately but clearly say no: "I'm sorry. I will not be able to answer your request."

3. You can work toward a compromise: "I can attempt to satisfy part of your concern or request."

Try to emphasize the positive things you can do. Then be sure to actually do what you said you will do.

As you begin to get a handle on the mind-set of each social style, you can learn to relate and communicate more effectively. As you gain a deeper understanding of social style, you can start to identify some of the gender stereotypes you have embraced. Once you realize that many of the differences you have attributed to gender are actually due to social style, you will begin to improve the way you relate to others.

For Your Improvement

Reflect on the following questions and write down your answers. Refer back to them as you work toward the improvement of your personal and professional relationships.

1. Who is the one person you are struggling with the most in your life right now, and what is his or her social style?

2. What steps can you take to create a more cohesive relationship with this person?

3. How can you adapt some of your own behavior to help this situation?

4. What else have you learned from this chapter, and how could you effectively apply this information to your personal and professional life?

14

Listening to Improve Relationships

Communication is comprised of three basic elements. First are the actual words that people say. The content of the words could be casual, humorous, serious, or even mean. Surprisingly, words make up only about 7 percent of communication. John Powell, in his book *Why Am I Afraid to Tell You Who I Am?* describes five levels of verbal communication.

1. Small talk (superficial).

    "How are you?'

    "How's the weather where you are?"

    "Did you catch the football game last night?"

2. Factual conversation (no personal comments, little risk).

    "I bought a new four-wheel-drive truck."

    "Mary just had a new baby boy. His name is Jeremiah."

    "We're going on a vacation to Palm Springs."

3. Ideas and opinions (no real intimacy).

    "I'm tired of hearing political commercials on television."

    "I think abortion is wrong."

    "I'd like to decorate the house with a country theme."

4. Feelings and emotions (freedom to express real emotions).

    "I really don't appreciate it when you come home late for dinner."

    "I'm so mad at you, I could spit nails."

    "I just got news that I may be laid off, and I'm scared to death."

5. Deep insight (complete emotional and personal self-disclosure).

　　"I just got word that I have cancer. I don't want to die."

　　"I have never told anyone this, but I stole some money from you."

　　"I haven't been honest with you, but I want to start today."

The second part of communication involves the tone of voice or the emphasis that is placed on the words spoken. Consider these examples:

I never said Allison had an affair. [Someone else said it.]

I *never* said Allison had an affair. [I kept it a secret.]

I never *said* Allison had an affair. [I only implied it.]

I never said *Allison* had an affair. [I never mentioned her name.]

I never said Allison *had* an affair. [I only said she was thinking about it.]

I never said Allison had an *affair*. [I only said she was flirting.]

Tone of voice and emphasis on words is a subtle form of conveying a message. Tone and emphasis comprise about 38 percent of communication.

The actions of men are the best
interpreters of their thoughts.
—John Locke

The third and largest area of communication is made up of nonverbal behavior. This includes things like these:

　　how people walk (fast or slow)

　　how people talk (loud or quiet)

　　posture (ridged or relaxed)

　　eye contact (direct or indirect)

　　body gestures (many or few)

reaction to others (outgoing or restrained)

response to stress (anger or fear)

facial expressions (positive or negative)

This area of communication is often referred to as *body language*. It is the most powerful form of communication. People believe our body language more than they believe our tone of voice or the content of our words. Nonverbal behavior or actions form a whopping 55 percent of communication. To be effective listeners, we must attend to not only what is spoken but also the way it is spoken. We must notice whether the nonverbal actions match the spoken words.

Understanding Total Communication

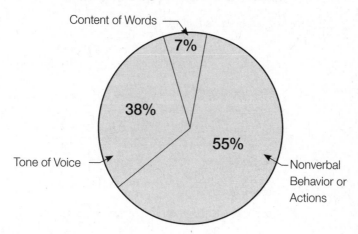

Barriers to Effective Listening

Listening to others is not always an easy task. We have just seen that we need to attend not only to their words but also to their tone of voice and nonverbal behavior. In addition to all that, we must be aware of what is happening in our own minds. We might not fully understand what others are trying to convey to us for several reasons:

disagreements and conflicting points of view

defensiveness

overeagerness to talk instead of listen

too many details and facts

pressure to make a decision or answer a question too quickly

not enough time to communicate clearly and calmly

fatigue

negative predisposition

boredom

impatience

flat tone of voice and lack of nonverbal communication

putting words in others' mouths or finishing their sentences

contradicting without listening

The two words *information* and *communication*
are often used interchangeably, but they signify
quite different things. Information is giving
out; communication is getting through.
—Sydney J. Harris

Benefits to Listening Attentively

- It can provide you with the facts and information you need.

- It lets other people know you are interested and concerned about what they are saying.

- It allows you time to determine other people's social style.

- It gives agitated and angry people an opportunity to vent their feelings and be heard.

- It exposes errors or misunderstandings that need to be corrected or restated.

- It offers polite respect to overbearing or hostile people without responding in kind.

- It helps you make wise decisions and respond appropriately.

- It helps you determine people's assumptions, perceptions, needs, expectations, and attitude.

Listening for People's Needs

Abraham Maslow suggested a seven-step evaluation of the driving motivation behind human behavior and actions. Considering these needs will help you become a more effective listener and will enrich your communication with friends, family, and coworkers. When you listen to people, try to determine if they need anything related to...

- *physical requirements*: food, drink, shelter, sex, sleep, or recovery from injury or illness

- *safety*: protection from violence or chaos, a sense of order or stability, absence of fear or anxiety, or a sense of order in a daily routine

- *belonging and love*: interactions with a spouse or mate, support from others during stressful times, harmonious family relationships, sense of belonging to a group, or close friendships

- *esteem*: respect from peers, mastery or proficiency in work or daily routine, or reputation or eminence in a particular field

- *self-actualization*: self-fulfillment or using one's capacities to their fullest

- *knowledge and understanding*: deep wisdom or understanding in a particular field or the development of a new system for explaining the world around us

- *aesthetics*: beauty and creativity

Building a Solid Foundation for Listening

Regardless of your social style or the social style of those you communicate with, you can improve your listening skills. Active listening is a whole-person attempt to understand what other people think and feel. It makes you an active part of the process. When other people truly feel heard, you know you have engaged in active listening. If you want to be an active listener, practice these skills.

Repeat what you heard. Be sure you are both on the same page and understanding the issue at hand. This will let the person know you are interested in approaching the topic of her concern. It will also increase your understanding.

Ask open-ended questions. "How do you think the issues should be handled?" "Do we need to talk about anything else now?" "What can I do to help resolve this problem?" "What type of information can I give you?" "Could you share with me your thinking about this subject?"

Ask for clarification. If you think the person has shared something that is incorrect or inaccurate, you need to clarify. Try not to challenge her statement in a threatening or sarcastic manner. Attempt to speak with an impartial tone of voice.

Clarify critical issues. Here are a dozen questions that can help you get to the heart of a conversation:

"What do you want from me?"

"How would you like to see things change?"

"What are your needs or desires?"

"How do you see me contributing?"

"What are your expectations?"

"How can I help in this matter?"

"What would you like to see done?"

"How would you like to see the future look?"

"What would you like me to do differently?"

"Is there a way I could change to help the situation?"

"What advice would you give me?"

"What can I do to make amends?"

Make statements rather than asking questions. If the conversation becomes stressful, attempt to make more *I* statements and ask fewer *you* questions. Under a tense situation, questions can come across like heat-seeking missiles that imply blame. Rather than asking, "Who gave you permission to go through my things?" try saying, "I see you've gone through my mail."

Maintain eye contact. This will send the message that you want the person to continue talking or explaining her thoughts. This will help encourage her to open up and be honest with you. People usually do not trust and are suspicious of those who do not look at them when communicating.

Listen with your body. Nod your head at appropriate comments. This conveys that you understand. Try not to cross your arms or legs and lean back. Putting your hands behind your head can come across as being smug. Lean slightly forward as a sign of interest.

Use encouraging words. Certain phrases help to create more open communication.

"No kidding."

"How interesting."

"I'm happy to hear that."

"Good!"

"Great!"

"I see."

"I understand."

"This sounds exciting. Tell me more."

"I'd be interested to hear what you have to say about this."

"Could you share your point of view with me?"

Try to stay away from loaded questions. A *why* question tends to sound accusatory. It can make people defensive. Instead of asking, "Why do you feel so angry?" try saying, "Tell me about your feelings over this matter."

Don't be afraid of silence. Conversations may include awkward silences. Many people think they must fill this void by saying something. Resist that urge. The silence gives the other person time to gather her thoughts or come up with new information. If you speak too soon, you may miss a very important bit of information.

Control your internal and external responses. Don't get defensive if someone is frustrated with you or your behavior. Don't tell yourself that you are being attacked. Instead, listen objectively without trying to solve the problem. Just make the other person feel heard.

Actually listen. Silence your mind and your thoughts and concentrate on what is being said. Don't formulate your response while someone is talking to you. Try to resist interrupting or interjecting, and don't finish other people's sentences.

Make notes. This will often cause the speaker to open up. This technique helps you to remember key facts, it carries the message that you are interested, and it gives you something to do during awkward silences that sometimes occur.

If you want to improve your listening skills, you will need to invest some time in the process. Listening is like any other skill: When you practice it often enough and do it well, you master it. Make a commitment today to become a better listener, and people won't have to keep asking you, "Can you hear me now?"

For Your Improvement

Reflect on the following questions and write down your answers. Refer back to them as you work toward the improvement of your personal and professional relationships.

1. What specific aspect of listening do you struggle with the most?

2. What steps can you take to become a better listener and communicator?

3. What else have you learned from this chapter, and how could you effectively apply this information to your personal and professional life?

15

Communication Crises

The wall of silence between Cory and Megan had been growing for months. No longer did they have fiery outbursts or heated arguments. Those had stopped weeks ago. Now, there was only the growing chill of indifference.

Cory no longer said goodbye. He just quietly headed for the door and went to work. Megan knew he was walking out but pretended not to notice. Both of them felt hurt and angry. Cory thought, *All I am is a paycheck. She doesn't appreciate how hard I work.* Megan choked back the tears and thought, *He doesn't even know I exist. He hasn't talked to me for days. How can I live with someone who doesn't love me?*

Cory and Megan were experiencing a crisis in their communication. This crisis did not arise because of gender differences. It didn't even occur because they had different social styles. It came about because they are part of the human race. The emotional forces within all of us make honest dialogue complicated.

Communication can be positive or negative. John F. Kennedy reminded us that some events could be considered dangerous and bring disaster. But those same events often bring opportunities for change, growth, and security.

It has been said that a problem well stated is a problem half solved. Let's look for a moment at the forces that cause communication crises. Cory and Megan experienced a series of events that brought about their cold silence.

Events and habits like these are never the real causes of communication problems:

forgetting to do something for the other person

speaking a harsh word

being late for dinner

not mowing the lawn

spending too much money

not disciplining the children

These behaviors get a lot of attention and can appear to start a conflict. But lurking in the shadows around the actual event are *thoughts* like these:

beliefs (rational or irrational)

assumptions (reasonable or unreasonable)

needs (valid or invalid)

attitudes (positive or negative)

expectations (logical or illogical)

demands (fair or unfair)

perceptions (accurate or inaccurate)

The way we think about events like these prompts our behaviors—for better or worse.

The biggest lesson I have ever learned is the stupendous importance of what we think. If I knew what you think, I would know what you are, for your thoughts make you what you are; by changing our thoughts, we can change our lives.

—Dale Carnegie

When we respond negatively, the feeling of hurt emerges. It is followed by disappointment. That disappointment can give rise to anger or fear. Out of our anger grows frustration, resentment, and depression. Out of our fear grows concern, worry, and anxiety.

If I become angry with you or fearful of you, I will no longer trust you. If I can't trust you, I then begin to lose respect for you. Once I lose respect for you, I begin to resent you. Resentment can then grow into bitterness, and it can even develop into hatred. If Cory and Megan repeat the process over and over again, it can become a habit or lifestyle.

Take a look at the chart below. It demonstrates the influence of thinking on emotions. Notice the many factors that play into events and help form our perception of an event. Emotions surface as a result of our perceptions.

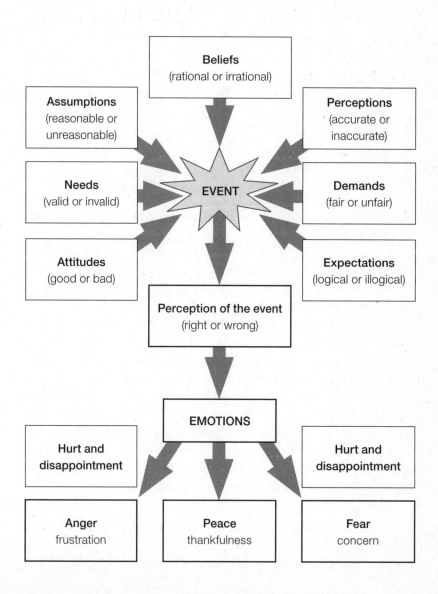

We all have a strong desire to be right, and we often believe that others are wrong. The drive to be right will cause us to discredit other people or put them in their place.

As communication breaks down, we no longer trust other people and their motives. We tend to judge ourselves by our motives, but we judge others by their behavior. In our twisted way of thinking, the more we downgrade other people with criticism, the more we upgrade ourselves. We can justify our feelings and thoughts as right and theirs as wrong.

Incredibly, the drive to be right is so strong that people are willing to destroy marriages, lose jobs, or break up churches just to prove their case. The compulsion to sacrifice others to validate our own egos is frightening. We should be amazed at the way people plot against others, persecute them, misrepresent them, or simply gossip about them.

A long habit of not thinking a thing wrong, gives
it a superficial appearance of being right.
—Thomas Paine

If I no longer trust or respect you, I will be very careful about what I say to you—or I might not say anything at all. When this happens, our relationship begins to die. Being silent or treating someone as a nonperson will destroy any bond.

When we treat people this way, they become apathetic or cynical. They could also respond with envy, competitiveness, or hostility. Both parties then begin to feel the impending death of the relationship. The relationship will not be saved unless one individual becomes courageous enough to address issues truthfully. Speaking truth is sometimes dangerous. You could be attacked, criticized, ignored, misrepresented, or mocked. On the other hand, truth spoken gracefully can restore, heal, and renew relationships.

Speaking the truth is liberating. It releases pent-up emotions, it invigorates us, and it restores the self-respect we lost when we didn't share what we believed about the relationship.

You will know the truth, and the truth will make you free.
—John 8:32

When we take the initiative to speak the truth in love, we experience an inner peace. We can be at harmony with ourselves, with others, and with God. Truthful and honest people become more and more thankful for everything in life. Truthfulness also helps them to become more accepting of others and of difficult situations in life. The end result is an amazing flow of happiness with life in general.

So where are you in this process? Do you think your problems are the result of gender differences? Or that maybe your difficulties are the consequence of your social style or the different social style of others?

Have you been thinking you're right and others are wrong? Are you willing to destroy relationships to justify your actions and beliefs? Have you been experiencing a loss of trust in some people, leading to a lack of respect for them? Has a root of bitterness sprung up and produced the fruit of hatred?

Have you been filled with anger and fear, which produce depression and anxiety? How long do you want this to continue? Do you want to carry a broken relationship with you to the grave? Are you tired of all the negative feelings you have been holding inside? Is it time for you to deal honestly with truth?

People change only when they hurt enough to change. Have you come to that point in life? If you have, take courage and stick your neck out. Take the initiative. Stop waiting for others to solve your dilemmas. You will feel better about yourself, and you might even turn danger into opportunity.

You gain strength, courage, and confidence
by every experience in which you really stop
to look fear in the face. You must do the
thing which you think you cannot do.

—Eleanor Roosevelt

For Your Improvement

Reflect on the following questions and write down your answers. Refer back to them as you work toward the improvement of your personal and professional relationships.

1. What are some negative patterns of communication that you regularly return to?

2. What steps could you take today to start breaking those patterns?

3. What else have you learned from this chapter, and how could you effectively apply this information to your personal and professional life?

16

Common Communication Questions

Dear Bob and Kim,

I've noticed lately that people keep saying to me things like "What did you say?" "Would you go over that again?" "Would you please repeat that?"

At first I thought I was dealing with a bunch of deaf people. But now, I'm wondering if I have some kind of problem. Do you have any suggestions that might help me? I'm very frustrated.

Dear Frustrated,

As people grow older they sometimes gradually do lose their hearing. If people are walking away from you when you start speaking, they may miss the first few words of your sentence. At home, one person may be in the living room, and the other one may be in the kitchen. The husband speaks in what he feel is a normal volume. But his wife hears some kind of mumbled sound and says, "What?" This irritates him, and he may say the sentence again in a stronger way. She gets upset because of his tone of voice...Welcome to the real world. In this situation, don't get irritated. The other person most likely didn't hear you. Simply gain eye contact and repeat your question or statement again with a smile. This will usually solve the issue.

However, the problem may not lie with the listener. You may have a habit of speaking softer at the end of your sentences. Visually, your sentence might look like this:

"Did you go to the mall with Sally?"

If your voice drops in volume, the natural response will be, "What did you say?" Ask a family member or a close friend to listen carefully as you speak to see if you are lowering your voice. Become conscious of the way you end your sentences. Practice speaking with the same volume for all of your comments.

Or you may be running words together. This is a common habit. Do you expect people to understand when you say "Howzitgoin?" or "You shudabener" or "Wherdjaseeit"?

Good communication is as stimulating as
black coffee, and just as hard to sleep after.
—Anne Morrow Lindbergh

Some people talk with their hand in front of their mouth. They might be unsure of what they are saying, they might be afraid they have bad breath, or they might be embarrassed about the color of their teeth or the fact that they wear braces. Talking with food or gum in your mouth doesn't help.

Try articulating your words more clearly. Instead of speaking in a tight-lipped manner, open your mouth a little wider and clearly speak your words. Practice reading out loud this version of the story of the Prodigal Son. Try to read it clearly. You will have to concentrate on moving your lips and pronouncing each word plainly.

Melody in F

Feeling footloose and frisky, a feather-brained fellow
Forced his fond father to fork over the farthings,
And flew far to foreign fields
And frittered his fortune feasting fabulously with faithless
    friends.
Fleeced by his fellows in folly and facing famine,
He found himself a feed-flinger in a filthy farm yard.
Fairly famishing, he fain would have filled his frame
With foraged food from fodder fragments.
"Fooey, my father's flunkies fare far finer,"
The frazzled fugitive forlornly fumbled, frankly facing fact.
Frustrated by failure and filled with foreboding,
He fled forthwith to his family. Falling at his father's feet,
    he forlornly fumbled,
"Father, I've flunked and fruitlessly forfeited family fellowship
    favor."
The farsighted father, forestalling further flinching,
Frantically flagged the flunkies to

Fetch a fatling from the flock and fix a feast.
The fugitive's faultfinding brother frowned
On fickle forgiveness of former folderol.
But the faithful father figured,
"Filial fidelity is fine, but the fugitive is found!
What forbids fervent festivity?
Let the flags be unfurled! Let fanfares flare!"
The father's forgiveness formed the foundation
For the former fugitive's future fortitude!

Dear Bob and Kim,

My friends tell me I talk too fast. They say I speak 180 words a minute with gusts up to 230 words. I don't know why I do it. I sort of monopolize conversations, and my friends can't get a word in edgewise. They have nicknamed me Windy.

Dear Windy,

Start by slowly taking three deep breaths and letting them out slowly before you start speaking. This will help you relax and give you a moment to gather your thoughts together. You might ask yourself, *Is this actually important? Would these people want me to add it to the conversation?* If not, it might be good to keep your mouth and thoughts in control.

The problem with communication is the
illusion that it has been accomplished.
—George Bernard Shaw

Some people talk fast because they are afraid no one will listen to them very long. They try to get all their thoughts out before someone walks away. Or their speedy talking may be the result of the home they were brought up in. In some families, everyone talks fast—and sometimes they all talk at the same time. They sound as if they're in a battle to see who can control the conversation and get their point across.

Anxiety can also cause people to talk fast. They might be fearful about something, or they could be frustrated and angry. Fear and anger can be driving forces that speed up the tempest of talk. Are you fearful about something? Are you hurt or angry because of some event?

To help you slow down, try the dot-dot method. After each sentence you speak out loud, say *dot-dot* silently. This will add a natural pace to your speaking. To practice this, pick up any book and start reading the sentences out loud. After each sentence, silently add *dot-dot*. If you do this every day for a few minutes, you will become conscious of the pace of your words. This new habit will give you more confidence when speaking.

A couple verses from the book of Proverbs and one from the book of Ecclesiastes might be good to commit to memory:

- "Watch your tongue and keep your mouth shut, and you will stay out of trouble" (Proverbs 21:23).

- "Wise words satisfy like a good meal; the right words bring satisfaction. The tongue can bring death or life; those who love to talk will reap the consequences" (Proverbs 18:20-21).

- "[There is] a time to be quiet and a time to speak" (Ecclesiastes 3:7).

Dear Bob and Kim,

I sometimes get the feeling that people don't want to talk to me. I want to communicate well, but I take a long time to get my point across. Other people seem to be able to say what they want to quickly, but my pace is more like a snail.

Dear Snail,

Several things could be going on. The people you are talking to may be under a lot of pressure to get some task done. They may be preoccupied with a deadline, or they might be emotionally tied up with a family problem or a personal illness issue. Try to understand the burdens people are carrying or the stress they're under.

The right to be heard does not automatically
include the right to be taken seriously.
—Hubert H. Humphrey

People's nonverbal body language will reveal whether they are uncomfortable with a conversation. If you see them tapping their fingers, you may be talking too slow or taking too long to get to the point. If they don't look at you when you talk, they are probably looking for someone, or they may be looking for a way out. They could also disagree with what you are saying but not want to speak up and share their thoughts. Sometimes when people want a conversation to end, they begin backing away from you. They may have some other engagement they need to go to, or they may not want to discuss the issue, or you may simply have bad breath.

Another issue might be that you actually talk too slow. You may be using too many pauses between your sentences or saying *and, um, uh,* or *ya know* too much. The pauses or words could indicate that you don't have your thoughts in order and you are giving yourself time to think.

Some people think they have to speak thoroughly and perfectly about a topic. Because of this they become too wordy, analytical, or precise. The listener gets lost in complicated explanations and technical details.

If you want to pick up the pace of your talking, try these ideas:

- Stay with one topic at a time. Don't mix a lot of random thoughts into your conversation, or listeners will have a difficult time trying to follow your ramblings.

- Stick to the essentials. Leave out the trivia and unnecessary facts even though you love to think about them. In other words, try to get to the bottom line quickly instead of allowing people to get bored. If they want more facts, they will ask for them.

- Maintain eye contact with people when you talk to them. This will give you a good idea whether they are tracking with you.

- Attempt to keep your comments, questions, or statements short. Don't ramble on and on. This will help you focus your thoughts and will help people understand where you are coming from.

- Ask your mate or a good friend to monitor your conversations with other people. Tell them to let you know if you're talking too much, talking too slow, or boring people. Be prepared—this may be a very humbling experience!

- Interject some questions if you think the person you are speaking to is not totally in tune with you.

    "What do you think?"

"Are you busy today? You seem preoccupied."

"Is this a bad time for you?"

"Do you have a few moments to talk?"

- If people close their eyes for a long time, you may have put them to sleep.

Dear Bob and Kim,

When I start talking with people, I feel short of breath. I don't know if I just need more oxygen or what. I find myself feeling like I'm gasping for air.

Wise men talk because they have something to
say; fools, because they have to say something.

—Plato

Dear Breathless,

When people are out of breath when they speak, they may be nervous. This causes them to take shallow breaths with their upper chests instead of breathing deeply from their diaphragms. Sloppy breathing habits are easy to develop.

We take about 23,000 breaths a day. Much of this breathing is shallow rather than deep. Shallow breathing does not bring sufficient oxygen into the body. One of the first signs of not taking in enough oxygen is the onset of headaches. The two go together. In fact, studies have shown that individuals who experience cluster headaches can usually eliminate them by breathing in oxygen for about 15 minutes.

To practice deep breathing, lie down on your back. Draw your knees up and allow them to spread apart slightly. Begin to relax and breathe deeply. Slowly draw in your breath to the count of six. Hold your breath for the count of six. Then slowly let your breath out to the count of six.

To help you breathe deeply, place a book on your stomach. Breathe in with your abdominal muscles, causing the book to rise. As you breathe out, the book will lower with your stomach.

To practice breathing deeply while sitting up, place both of your hands on your stomach and slowly breathe in and out to the count of six as before. By having your hands on your stomach, you can feel whether you are breathing deeply. For a good exchange of air while you are walking, breathe in with four short separate inhales. Do not hold your breath. Immediately after drawing in the fourth breath, let out your air with four separate short exhales.

If you are running and want a good exchange of air, use two quick inhales and two quick exhales. Breathing in and out to the count of two will give you sufficient air while you are running and will help you to run longer distances. Counting to two—in and out—will also help you concentrate on your breathing rather than your running. You won't run very far without enough oxygen.

Learning to breathe deeply not only gives us more air but also gives us confidence when speaking to others. It helps us relax.

Dear Bob and Kim,

I am a large man with a deep voice. My family, friends, and coworkers sometimes tell me I talk too loud. I'm confused because I think I use a normal tone of voice. What do I do?

Dear Mr. Loudmouth,

At least you won't have to worry about speaking to a large audience without a microphone—you seem to have one built in. Having a strong voice might be advantageous if you are a policeman or newscaster. The good news is that you are not alone. Many men who have deep voices struggle with their volume control.

> Her voice was ever soft, gentle, and
> low, an excellent thing in woman.
> —William Shakespeare

The bad news is that people with loud, deep voices tend to intimidate those who don't have deep voices. If you have a loud voice when you are talking normally, what do you sound like when you are upset or angry? Do you blow the house down?

To help you reduce the volume, ask your spouse or a friend for help.

Practice reading aloud from a book or a newspaper. Use your normal speaking voice—the one people say is too loud.

Have your spouse or friend say, "A little softer." Keep turning the volume down until he says, "That's great. Right there." Of course, this may be uncomfortable because you have developed a habit of speaking loudly. Creating a new habit of speaking at a more moderate volume may take a while.

Remember, you are not trying to deny who you are or discredit the voice God gave you. Your volume adjustment is to help those around you feel more comfortable and less intimidated. This can reduce misunderstanding and bring more harmony into your relationships.

As a side note, consider having your hearing tested. Sometimes people who are losing their hearing tend to raise their voices.

Dear Bob and Kim,

When I start talking, things don't seem to come out right. I don't know if I have marbles in my brain or marbles in my mouth.

Dear Marble Mouth,

Often people do not think about how they are going to pronounce words when they start talking. Also, regional accents and colloquialisms (*y'all, yoos gize,* and the like) and foreign words and accents can hinder understanding.

If you continually find people looking at you like dogs do when they hear an unusual sound, you should probably try to speak more clearly. Practice your speaking before a mirror, and imagine you are speaking to a person or a group.

Make sure your lips are limber. Pucker up and slightly overemphasize words that have the *oo* sound, such as *tool* or *booth*. Imitate a smile and overemphasize words that have the *ee* sound, like *deed* or *keep*. Then alternate back and forth between saying "two deer, two deer, two deer." (Avoid doing this in public, or people *will* believe you have marbles in your head.)

Speaking of marbles in your head, think about what you are going to say before you open your mouth. Or as others have said, "Put your brain in gear before you put your mouth in motion." In front of the mirror, practice sharing an idea out loud. Pretend that you are speaking to a friend. Try to make your point in just a few words and less than 30 seconds. This will help you gather your thoughts (or arrange your marbles) in a way that makes sense and sounds good. If it doesn't sound good to you, it probably won't make sense to someone else.

These sentence starters can help you organize and share your thoughts:

"Did you hear about...?"

"I remember..."

"When I was a child..."

"What is your opinion about...?"

"Get this..."

"What do you think about...?"

Dear Bob and Kim,

I don't know what to do with my voice. Everyone says it's high-pitched. What's the problem? Can I change that?

Dear High Pitch,

Sometimes people's voices are high-pitched when they are nervous or stressed. Reducing your stress can help to lower the pitch.

Changing the pitch of your voice can be helpful in several ways. Studies indicate that when a person's voice rises to a higher pitch, listeners begin to think that the speaker is out of control and react negatively. For example, teachers and their classes have been observed through two-way mirrors. An interesting phenomenon occurs when a teacher's voice rises. Disruptive classroom behavior rises in direct proportion to the rise in the teacher's voice. If the pitch level lowers, the disruptive behavior lowers. Teachers, parents, and supervisors can increase their effectiveness by lowering their pitch and measuring their words.

Communication leads to community, that is, to understanding, intimacy, and mutual valuing.
—Rollo May

Our parents demonstrated this a long time ago. When they slowly and deeply said, "If...you...do that...*one...more...time...*" The message came across loud and clear even though they were not yelling. People with a lower pitch seem to come across as more authoritative and stronger in their personality.

You can test your pitch by using the phrase *uh-huh* in a normal tone. If the *uh-huh* sounds higher than your normal pitch, you are probably increasing your pitch more than necessary. Remember, lower your pitch and measure your words. Try to observe the reaction of those you speak with.

Dear Bob and Kim,

I feel like such an idiot. People introduce themselves to me, and within the next ten seconds I can't remember who I'm talking with. Is there any hope?

Dear Forgetful,

Join the club. You are certainly not alone in this area. People are often so preoccupied that names don't seem to register, especially several names at once.

Most memory experts suggest that you repeat people's names out loud or ask them to spell their names for you. This helps you set aside your other thoughts and focus on people and what they are saying.

You can also ask for a business card or write their name down. Try to associate their name with something familiar, like Bill from Buffalo. (But you might stop short of saying "Buffalo Bill"!)

When you can't remember someone's name, just say something like this: "Please forgive me—I should know your name, but my forgetter is working overtime." Most people will gladly repeat their name for you. However, you may run across the occasional folks who will get upset because you don't remember their name. Take it in stride. It happens to all of us.

Don't you love it when people come up to you and say their name before you start talking? It saves a great deal of embarrassment. You can serve others by developing this habit when you greet them.

Work out a mutual agreement with your spouse, friend, or coworker. If your friend begins talking with someone and does not introduce her to you, that's your signal. Your friend has probably forgotten her name. Introduce yourself. When she says her name, your friend will be off the hook.

Dear Bob and Kim,

Parties and social gatherings are difficult for me. I'm not into small talk about the weather, food, or sports. I start thinking about other things I could be doing rather than talking about the color of someone's tie. I just wish people would get to the point and say something important.

Dear Bottom-Liner,

No one is an island. We all have to attend social gatherings. Some people (Amiables and Expressives) get energized by being around people. Analyticals and Drivers can do fine in social settings, but interaction can drain them. They are energized by accomplishing tasks.

A few suggestions might help. First, don't be selfish. If your spouse or friend wants to socialize, don't be a stick-in-the-mud. The world doesn't have to revolve around you and your needs. Think about other people's needs and desires too. You won't die or catch a disease if you go to a party. Be willing to go and to maintain an upbeat, selfless attitude.

It is as easy to draw back a stone, thrown with force from the hand, as to recall a word once spoken.
—Menander

If you are task-oriented, change your thinking about the social event. Think positively and take on the social gathering as one of your tasks. Determine to make it a good evening. Set a goal of finding someone you can get to know and help in some fashion. Take note of ways you can make a contribution. Maybe you could help the host and hostess serve the guests or clean up after the party. Maybe someone is hurting, and you could be like a breath of fresh air to him.

And yes, you may have to endure a few minutes of small talk. When you do this cheerfully, people will realize you are not aloof. You are a normal person. You are approachable. You have some fun stories to share. Become alert to people's expressions, tone of voice, and nonverbal behavior. Maintain eye contact and listen for attitudes and feelings that go beyond words. After the small talk, you may well find opportunities to get into more significant issues like politics, the economy, world events, religion, and other areas of interest for you.

> We who lived in concentration camps can remember
> the men who walked through the huts comforting
> others, giving away their last piece of bread. They may
> have been few in number, but they offer sufficient
> proof that everything can be taken from a man but
> one thing: the last of the human freedoms—to choose
> one's attitude in any given set of circumstances, to
> choose one's own way. The man who never does
> anything he doesn't like, rarely likes anything he does.
> —Victor Frankl

Dear Bob and Kim,

Some people are like clams. They never open up in conversations or contribute any of their thoughts. How do I help them to participate in discussions?

Dear Crowbar,

Drivers and Expressives share their thoughts and emotions more easily than Analyticals and Amiables, who tend to be more reserved.

Analytical people will sometimes hesitate to share because they don't want to make inaccurate statements. They need time to think through their thoughts and slowly come to conclusions they feel good about. People may be quiet because they want more information before they respond and say the wrong thing.

Amiables can often be quiet as well. They too are hesitant to share with others but for a different reason. They may be reserved because they want to save relationships at all costs. They don't want to say anything that could be misunderstood and sever associations. They would rather carry their own hurts or sufferings than share something that could cause conflict. They tend to seek peace at all costs.

It is important not to be pushy and try to pry thoughts and feelings from Analyticals and Amiables. They do not appreciate people who come on too strong. They need facts and assurances that if they express their feelings, they won't be attacked, belittled, or rejected. People who are quiet and seem withdrawn need encouragement, praise, and understanding. They need to understand why sharing is important and how it will enhance their relationships rather than destroy them. They will feel free to share only after they know what is expected of them.

One of the basic causes for all the trouble in the world today is that people talk too much and think too little. They act impulsively without thinking. I always try to think before I talk.
—Margaret Chase Smith

If a tortoise's head was withdrawn, how would you get it to come out of its shell? Would pounding on its shell and yelling at it help? Or would kind tones and soft words be more likely to do the trick? Similarly, positive phrases like these are more likely to help quiet people open up their clam shell:

"I want your advice."

"I need your assistance."

"I'd love to hear about…"

"Tell me your opinion of…"

"Please share with me…"

"What do you think about…"

Dear Bob and Kim,

I get along with most people, but some drive me crazy. I have the hardest time with boring people. In fact, the word *bore* is too mild for some people; they are more like pneumatic drills. How do I survive them?

Dear Bored to Tears,

Some people love to hear the sound of their own voices. They are constantly talking and talking. In fact, they often enter rooms mouth first.

Many of the people who talk continually are actually suffering from a lack of self-confidence. They have a hard time dealing with silence and feel that they must fill any gaps in conversations. In a way, they try to control discussions, which often revolve around their accomplishments, how people like them, and how their needs are going to be met. Self-confident people can deal with silence. They are okay with not sharing all of their thoughts and feelings with others, and they respect other people's time.

Henry Ford said, "A bore is a fellow who opens his mouth and puts his feats in it." Jonathan Swift suggested, "Few wild beasts are more to be dreaded than a talking man having nothing to say."

Boredom has another side, however. You may be bored because people aren't interested in what you're saying and doing. As others have said, "We often forgive those who bore us; we cannot forgive those whom we bore."

Maybe the issue is that you are a bottom-line person and you don't have the patience to listen to long-drawn-out facts and details. The question then becomes, whose problem is it? You might need to become more tolerant and less hurried. We can easily forget that not everyone thinks and responds the same way we do. We need to remember that the world doesn't revolve around us and our style of behavior.

If you encounter people who eat up a lot of your time with mindless chatter, try this:

- Stand up when they come into your office. Don't give the allusion that they can just come in and sit down and shoot the breeze.

- Before they start talking, say something like this: "Carl, it's good to see you. I've only got five minutes to talk. I have another engagement."

- If they involve you in an unnecessary conversation, take a deliberate look at your watch and say, "I just noticed the time. I need to deal with another matter. Would you please excuse me?"

Dear Bob and Kim,

Sometimes I don't feel like people pay attention to me—my boss, my coworkers, and even my family. How can I get them to listen to me?

Dear Now Hear This!

The American military may provide us with an answer. A private may speak to a general only if he follows the right procedure. The private must set up an appointment, or the opportunity must present itself. When that happens, he must respect the general's time and position.

The more elaborate our means of
communication, the less we communicate.
—Joseph Priestley

The next step is very important. The private must say something like this: "Sir, do I have permission to speak frankly?" Rarely will a general say no unless he is under a great deal of stress or pressed for time. Normally, the general will respond, "You have permission, private."

The private can then respectfully share what is on his mind even if it disagrees with the general's point of view. The general may respond positively, neutrally, or negatively, depending on the circumstances. But regardless of the general's response, the private has been heard.

This example provides some suggestions for communicating with superiors. But what about coworkers, friends, and family?

Write down the key points you would like to share with the person. Commit them to memory or keep a copy with you. Then look for an opportunity to talk with her. Try to find a time when neither of you are in a hurry and when you can speak privately. Ask if she has a moment to talk with you. If she says, "Sorry, not right now," set up a convenient time. If possible, avoid discussing heavy topics in your office or her office. Try to find neutral territory, like a restaurant or coffee shop. Better yet, go for a walk.

By going for a walk, you don't have to maintain eye contact, which is sometimes difficult. Walking lets off some of your nervous energy. It allows you to be alone with the individual where other people will not overhear the conversation. As you walk and talk, the problem is in front of both of you—your voices are going forward. This helps both of you remain positive and objective.

Dear Bob and Kim,

I have a nagging fear that if someone asks me a question, I may not have the answer. How can I eliminate this concern?

Dear Nagging Fear,

Who has all the answers? You can't possibly prepare yourself to answer every question that comes to you. People who ask you difficult questions don't have the answers either.

The only one who has the answer to every question is God. Relax a little. The universe will not stop moving if you can't respond to every question people ask you.

When people talk, listen completely.
Most people never listen.
—Ernest Hemingway

When we were younger, we seemed to need to be able to answer everyone's questions and engage their arguments. The older and wiser we get, the easier we can say, "I don't know. That's a good question."

Often people who ask difficult questions don't actually want an answer. They just want to make some sort of statement or express their own bias or pet peeve. Let them share their thoughts and then say, "Thanks for sharing your thoughts. That's an interesting point of view. Can we continue where we left off?" Then get back on track with your conversation.

Dear Bob and Kim,

Some people are annoying and hard to get along with. How do I survive working and living with them? How do I troubleshoot relationships with irritating people?

Dear Troubleshooter,

Welcome to reality. You will always be around some difficult people. You will not be able to get rid of them. In fact, get ready for a shock: You may be an annoying person for someone else.

What do annoying people look like? Go to your local mall or grocery store, and you will see lots of them.

- They are impatient. Do you get upset with drivers who go too slow or cut you off? Have you ever accidentally cut someone off?

- They wander down conversational rabbit trails. Have you ever strayed from the main focus of a conversation?

- They have bad habits, like continually clearing their throat, rattling change in their pockets, or picking their nose. You don't have any bad habits, do you?

- They are late for appointments and don't complete projects. Have you always been on time and finished your tasks?

- They are fearful of what others might think. We would worry less about what others think of us if we realized how seldom they do.

- They get angry at little picky things that don't matter in the big picture. Aren't you glad that you never get angry and always stay calm?

- They are forgetful and prone to exaggerate the truth. You are consistently honest and have a great memory, right?

- They don't communicate very well at work or home. That only leaves three people who communicate well: Bob, Kim, and you.

I'm sure you get the point. Everyone annoys someone at some time. That is why we wrote *How to Deal with Annoying People.* In that book we attempted to describe the social styles and the way they can get along with each other. It also includes about 70 pages of beneficial information about conflict resolution.

17

What You Need to Work On

I would like to close this book by summarizing ways you can improve your relationships, regardless of gender. This will provide you with some insight on what people might think of you because of your social style and what you can do to make yourself easier to work with and live with. Everyone has blind spots. Those who are unaware of theirs are generally unaware they are unaware and need to be reminded of them.

If You Are an Analytical

You are a technique specialist. You're organized and careful to do things right. Your dry but witty sense of humor is one of your strong points. You tend to be loyal to others, and people appreciate the fact that you are self-disciplined. You have a lot of things going for you, but you could improve in a few areas.

You tend to overanalyze things. This can make people crazy, especially Drivers and Expressives. If you want to improve in this area, once you have the facts, make your decision!

Your standards are often too high for people. I know this may be a stretch for you, but if you want to improve, lighten up. People often view you as unsociable and withdrawn. To put it bluntly, people see you as a stick-in-the-mud at times. Your focus is often on completing tasks, and your Expressive and Amiable loved ones would like to spend more personal time with you.

In the midst of conflict, you tend to withdraw and avoid undesirable people and situations. Drivers and Expressives want to work through conflicts on the spot, and Amiables will feel abandoned if you withdraw. Stretch yourself to stay engaged during conflict and try to work through it constructively and encourage others to do the same.

> You will either step forward into growth
> or you will step back into safety.
> —Abraham Maslow

You tend to be more practical than romantic, and your romantic counterparts may not feel that you show enough passion. Try to think of ways you can develop and show more passion and romance.

You come across as a little too serious at times. Loosen up and have some fun! Yes, focus and seriousness are sometimes necessary, but you can take this too far. If you live or work with an Expressive, this can be a problem. Expressives want to have fun and live spontaneously, so if you want to get along better with them, try to be more creative and less predictable.

Try not to be critical and negative. Your tendency is to think through all of the details and everything that could go wrong so you can make proper contingency plans. That's not a bad thing, but the way you approach it or present it can be viewed as negative. People can feel as if you're raining on their parade. Try taking a more positive approach to potential problems, especially when someone comes to you excited about an idea.

Try not to worry so much about imperfections. Not everyone will perform to your standards, and you often think that if you want something done right, you have to do it yourself. Learning to accept less than perfect performance from others and yourself will make life a lot easier on you.

> One of the marks of excellent people is that they
> never compare themselves with others. They only
> compare themselves with themselves and with
> their past accomplishments and future potential.
> —Brian Tracy

If You Are a Driver

You have a lot of vision, drive, and ambition. As a natural-born leader, you tend to gravitate toward responsibility and leadership roles. People appreciate and admire your productivity and determination. Learning to channel that drive and determination into the right areas will be a good challenge for you. Here are some specific ways you can improve your relationships.

You tend to come across as a bull in a china shop. In your quest to get things accomplished, you often roll over the top of people who, in your opinion, move too slowly, react too slowly, and make decisions too slowly. Think of ways you can be tactful instead of blunt and abrasive.

You naturally struggle with just sitting down and relaxing because you are always mindful of projects that need attention. If slowing yourself down is too much to ask, at least consider letting other people relax instead of expecting them to perform at your level. Your militant style at work and at home can add a lot of stress to others. Let the kids have fun and relax. Let your employees and coworkers sit down for five minutes and catch their breath.

You don't need a lot of praise and affirmation, but you may forget that other people do need these things, especially Amiables. Make a conscious effort to give positive feedback to people you live and work with so they don't feel as if they failed to meet your expectations.

Learn how to say "I was wrong" and "I'm sorry." You have a lot of pride to manage. You have a tough time admitting you could ever be wrong, and you may come across as a know-it-all. Even if you are absolutely sure of what you are talking about, practice saying, "I could be wrong, but I thought..." This will help you demonstrate some humility, which is not your strongest trait.

> Men are anxious to improve their circumstances,
> but are unwilling to improve themselves;
> they therefore remain bound.
>
> —James Allen

You need to work on tolerance as well. You are annoyed by perceived incompetence. Learn to exercise more patience with people and circumstances. Try to show some compassion and sensitivity to others. Because you are not a sensitive person, you can easily forget that others may be. Practice ways to show some sympathy and kindness in this area.

Take input from others and don't always assume you have the best answer. Ask people what they think and encourage others to join in conversations. Be aware that you tend to dominate conversations and that Amiables and Analyticals will get shut out because they won't fight for the floor. As a natural leader, take the lead in yielding the floor in conversations and asking other people about their opinions.

Lastly, be careful about being sarcastic. You can shred people's opinions and feelings, especially in conflict. If you don't get a handle on this, you could become unfeeling, cold, and caustic. This is an important area for you to improve if you want to have better relationships in life.

If You Are an Amiable

You are generally the most liked person in an organization or a group of friends because you try to avoid conflict and make everyone happy. People appreciate your kind and diplomatic disposition and your compassion.

I thought I could change the world. It took me a hundred years to figure out I can't change the world. I can only change Bessie. And honey, that ain't easy either.
—Annie Elizabeth Delany

You need to develop your ability to deal with conflict. Telling people how you really feel is difficult for you because you don't want to create conflict or stress. As a result, you often let people roll over the top of you, including your kids and coworkers. As a parent, you struggle with being a disciplinarian and will sometimes try to be more of a friend to your kids. Be aware of the importance of setting and enforcing boundaries with your children and people you supervise.

Watch out for your tendency to be passive-aggressive. When people make you angry or hurt you in some way, you would rather not confront them about it. As a result, you may resort to passive-aggressive behavior to get back at them. Remember that confronting people and issues can actually improve your relationships and not destroy them.

The truth is that there is nothing noble in being superior to somebody else. The only real nobility is in being superior to your former self.
—Whitney Young

Be willing to take a stand on important issues. Drivers and Expressives would rather you disagree with them than not have an opinion. You probably internalize other people's feelings, so remember, when they show anger or frustration, they aren't necessarily mad at you.

Practice making decisions faster. You tend to be indecisive because you would hate to make the wrong decision and create conflict. Stretch yourself because Drivers and Expressives struggle with people who are slow to make decisions.

You tend to prefer to watch and observe rather than actively engage. As a result, you can come across as blasé and indifferent. Try to show a little more passion and conviction about things that are important to the people you live and work with.

Try to stretch yourself in the risk-taking area as well. You tend to want to play it safe, and you may be missing out on some great opportunities and experiences by not taking occasional risks.

You would also benefit from trying to set more goals for yourself. You are not always the most motivated person in the world, and goal setting may help you in this area.

Change is difficult for you. You tend to resist change, and in a work environment, this can bring other people down. Even if you do like the changes people propose, you can come across as unenthusiastic about them. Be aware of the way people perceive your quiet disposition: They may think you are shy and compromising.

If You Are an Expressive

People love your sense of humor—you're the life of the party! You make people laugh, and you can be very enthusiastic and Expressive. People appreciate your appealing personality, charisma, and persuasive nature.

The strongest principle of growth lies in human choice.
—George Eliot

Consider reserving your opinion sometimes. You tend to let everyone know where you stand, and your ability to express your views is sometimes a little overwhelming. Back off a little, lower your voice, and find out what other people think.

Make a goal of improving your listening skills. You tend to interrupt, interject, and talk over the top of people, especially when you are angry or passionate about a subject. Practice listening intently and asking people questions. Try to not one-up their stories or make all of the conversations about you.

You come on pretty strong at times, and that can scare people off. You can also be a compulsive talker, and that turns people off at times as well. You exude a restless energy that can make Analyticals and Amiables uncomfortable.

You love getting involved in big, complicated projects, but you get bored easily and don't always follow through. Work on sustaining your focus, completing projects, and reaching your goals.

As a parent, you don't always listen to the whole story, and this frustrates your children. Hear them out, exercise some patience, and stay relaxed. You can be inconsistent with rules and discipline, and this will frustrate your spouse and children.

You sometimes forget your obligations and appointments, and this would be a good area to work on. Write things down. Use a PDA. Show up on time.

You probably dominate a lot of conversations and take center stage. Try to share the limelight with others so your friends don't begin to resent you. Resist the temptation to answer for people and tell them how to live their lives. Practice waiting for people to ask you for input before offering it.

The greatest choice we have is to think before we act and then take action toward our life goals every day. Our problems result not only from our lack of action, but from our action without thought.

—Denis Waitley

You make decisions very quickly—sometimes without all the facts and information you need. As a result, your decisions may appear rash. Remember to think before you act. And be willing to take things seriously once in a while. You are great at turning disaster into humor, but sometimes you would do well to put the jokes and humor on hold and deal with a serious issue. Make sure you are choosing appropriate times, places, and situations before you let your humor rip.

Lastly, remember your tendency to be emotional about things. Try to keep your emotions in check, especially in conflicts or when you are angry. It's okay to leave the room, take a deep breath, count to 100, and then come back and deal with the situation. Otherwise, you may end up saying things you regret later.

For Your Improvement

Reflect on the following questions and write down your answers. Refer back to them as you work toward the improvement of your personal and professional relationships.

1. What specific areas in your life have you identified that need improvement?

2. What steps can you take today to start making these improvements?

3. What else have you learned from this book, and how could you effectively apply this information to your personal and professional life?

Finding Your Social Style

To find your social style, look at the charts that follow and check the boxes that apply to you most.

ASK	TELL
☐ I tend to be reserved.	☐ I tend to be outgoing.
☐ I'm not very assertive.	☐ I am assertive.
☐ I make thoughtful decisions.	☐ I make quick decisions.
☐ I avoid confrontation.	☐ I don't mind confrontation.
☐ I am usually patient.	☐ I tend to be impatient.
☐ I reserve my opinions.	☐ I share my opinions.
☐ I tend to be easygoing.	☐ I tend to be intense.
☐ I talk softly and slowly.	☐ I talk fast and loudly.
☐ People say I'm shy or introverted.	☐ People say I'm friendly or ambitious.

Proceed to the chart on the next page and check the boxes that apply to you most.

TASK	RELATIONSHIP
☐ I guard my emotions.	☐ I share my emotions.
☐ I tend to be serious.	☐ I tend to be playful.
☐ I am usually on time.	☐ I am often late.
☐ I like to appear businesslike.	☐ I like to appear informal or casual.
☐ I'm strict about rules.	☐ I tend to be lenient.
☐ I like to work alone.	☐ I like to work with others.
☐ I am hard to get to know.	☐ I am easy to get to know.
☐ I like to work first and then play.	☐ I like to play first and then work.
☐ I am focused about my work.	☐ I get distracted and am more carefree.

In the first set of responses, which did you choose more often?

☐ Ask   ☐ Tell

In the second set of responses, which did you choose most often?

☐ Task   ☐ Relationship

If you selected Ask and Task, you are an Analytical.
If you selected Tell and Task, you are a Driver.
If you selected Ask and Relationship, you are an Amiable.
If you selected Tell and Relationship, you are an Expressive.

An Overview of Each Social Style
Analyticals—the Technique Specialists

Analyticals are precise, and they are experts in the area of technique. Analyticals have a strong sense of duty and obligation. They are driven by a forceful work ethic, and play does not come naturally to them. They are natural givers and often take on the role of parent or guardian for other people and organizations.

Analyticals tend to take on too much responsibility. They see themselves as conservators and tend to worry. They will save and store for the future, believing they cannot save too much. They are steadfast, reliable, and dependable. Here are some of the Analytical's greatest strengths:

deep and thoughtful

serious and purposeful

genius-prone

talented and creative

artistic or musical

philosophical and poetic

appreciative of beauty

sensitive to others

self-sacrificing

conscientious

idealistic

seeks ideal mate

Drivers—the Control Specialists

Drivers need to perform and be in control. They take pleasure in almost any kind of work because it involves activity. Idleness will destroy Drivers. They want to master everything they do. They speak with precision and little redundancy.

Drivers like new ideas, challenges, and competition. They have a passion for knowledge. They constantly search to answer the big questions of life. They can be overly forceful and may require too much from themselves and others. Drivers are haunted by the possibility of failure. They are self-controlled, persistent, and logical. Here are some of the Driver's strengths:

born leader

dynamic and active

compulsive need for change

must correct wrongs

strong-willed and decisive

not easily discouraged

unemotional

exudes confidence

can run anything

independent and self-sufficient

Amiables—the Support Specialists

Amiables are likeable people who support others. They work well with others and promote harmony. They are often wrapped up in causes. They like to work with words and often influence large groups through writing. They sometimes place unrealistic expectations on themselves and others. They will often romanticize experiences and relationships.

Amiables like to have direction. They often observe others and seek deep meaning in relationships and experiences. They prefer interaction to action. Amiables are compassionate with those who hurt. They are patient, they listen well, and they are filled with integrity. Here are some of the Amiable's greatest strengths:

low-key personality

easygoing and relaxed

calm, cool, and collected

patient and well-balanced

consistent

quiet but witty

sympathetic and kind

keeps emotions hidden

happily reconciled to life

all-purpose person

Expressives—the Social Specialists

Expressives are impulsive people who love to socialize. They like to try things that are new and different. They enjoy wandering, and they can easily break social ties. They like to live for the here and now. Expressives struggle with commitment and follow-through.

Expressives have happy and charismatic spirits and can endure hardships and trials easier than the other social styles can. Discomfort is just a new experience that they know will pass. They love to reminisce and enjoy belonging to social organizations. They are friendly, giving, and easygoing. Here are some of the Expressive's greatest strengths:

appealing personality

talkative, storyteller

life of the party

good sense of humor

memory for color

likes to touch

emotional and demonstrative

enthusiastic and expressive

cheerful and bubbly

curious

good on stage

lives in the present

changeable disposition

sincere heart

always a child

If you would like an in-depth look at each of the social styles and how they operate, pick up a copy of *How to Deal with Annoying People.* It will tell you which styles combine better as partners, how to lead each style, how to follow each style, how to adapt to get along with anyone, and much more. You can also find information about the social styles at www.HowToDeal WithAnnoyingPeople.com and www.MenAreSlobsWomenAreNeat.com.

Appendix B

Secondary Social Styles

As you determined your social style, you may have noticed that you seem to identify with some of the traits of a second social style. Don't worry—you are normal.

Most people have a secondary, less dominant style. Your secondary style is what makes you unique and sets you apart from others with that same style. Determining your secondary is similar to determining your primary social style. Let's look at an example.

After reviewing the lists in appendix A, Linda could easily see that she was a teller and was predominately task-oriented. She determined that her primary social style was Driver. To determine her secondary style, she reviewed these lists again and realized that she had none of the Ask traits, but she did have several of the Relationship traits. So her secondary style would be Tell with Relationship, which is an Expressive. Because her primary style is Driver and her secondary style is Expressive, she is an Expressive Driver. The secondary style describes the way you conduct your primary style. Linda would be somewhat Expressive in the way she behaves as a Driver.

Linda also went through the lists of strengths and weaknesses of each style and noticed that the Driver social style definitely described most of her strengths and weaknesses. The Expressive lists had many characteristics that described her as well, but not as predominately as the Driver characteristics. Since Linda had none of the characteristics described on the Ask list, we know that her secondary style would not be Amiable or Analytical (both are askers).

Had Linda selected all of the Ask characteristics instead of Tell, and her answers remained the same in the Task/Relationship list, her primary style would have been Analytical (Ask/Task). Since she possessed some of the Relationship characteristics, her secondary style would have been Amiable

(Ask/Relationship). If she possessed none of the Tell characteristics, we know that her secondary style would not have been Driver or Expressive.

When you combine the primary and secondary social styles, you will find 16 possible styles (primary styles are in all caps, and secondary styles are in lower case):

The Sixteen Social Style Combinations

Analytical ANALYTICAL	Analytical AMIABLE
Driver ANALYTICAL	Driver AMIABLE
Amiable ANALYTICAL	Amiable AMIABLE
Expressive ANALYITCAL	Expressive AMIABLE
Analytical DRIVER	Analytical EXPRESSIVE
Driver DRIVER	Driver EXPRESSIVE
Amiable DRIVER	Amiable EXPRESSIVE
Expressive DRIVER	Expressive EXPRESSIVE

This should help explain why you see yourself in more than one category. You have a primary style and a secondary style. Additionally, you are actually some of all four, even though you manifest the traits of predominately two of the social styles (see Appendix C).

Appendix C

You're Some of
All Four Social Styles

As you have been reading this book and identifying your social style, you may have seen characteristics in yourself from each social style category. That's because you are actually some of all four. In addition to your primary social style and secondary social style, you have glimpses of the remaining two social styles. The amount of each social style you reflect is what makes you so incredibly unique from others.

The pie chart below shows an example of a Driver with a secondary social style of Expressive. This person has very little Amiable and even less Analytical.

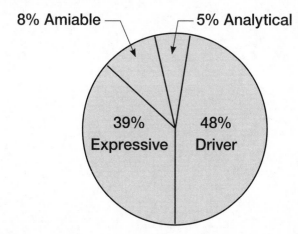

As a Driver with a lot of Expressive traits, this person would be very extroverted, confident, passionate, and focused on the big picture. She would also struggle with impatience.

When you create a mental pie chart of your social styles, consider learning how to demonstrate the positive behavior traits from the categories you are weakest in. You cannot choose your instinctual social style, but you can choose your behavior.

As a Driver, you may be prone to impatience. But you can choose the behavior traits of an Amiable or Analytical and become more patient. As an Amiable, you may be prone to avoiding conflict, but you can choose the behavior of an Expressive or a Driver and confront important issues. Regardless of your primary and secondary social style, you can develop the behaviors that don't come naturally to you.

Your personality will never reflect a perfectly balanced pie chart with an equal percentage of each social style, but you can certainly work on being more balanced. As you progress toward this goal, people will find you much easier to get along with.

Bibliography

Archer, John. "Sex Differences in Social Behavior." *American Psychologist* 51, 1996, 9.

Augsburger, David. *When Caring Is Not Enough.* Ventura, CA: Regal Books, 1983.

Barnett, R., and Rivers, C. *Same Difference: How Gender Myths Are Hurting Our Relationships, Our Children, and Our Jobs.* New York: Basic Books, 2004.

Baron-Cohen, Simon. *The Essential Difference: The Truth About the Male and Female Brain.* New York: Basic Book, 2003.

Blum, Deborah. *Sex on the Brain.* New York: Viking Press, 1997.

Bonnot, V., and Croizet, J. "Stereotype internalization and women's math performance: The role of interference in working memory." *Journal of Experimental Social Psychology* 43, no. 6, 2007, 857-66.

Brannon, Linda. *Gender: Psychological Perspectives.* Boston: Allyn & Bacon, 2007.

Cathcart, J. *The Acorn Principle.* New York: St. Martin's Griffin, 1998.

Ceci, Stephen. *Why Aren't More Women in Science? Top Researchers Debate the Evidence.* Washington DC: American Psychological Association, 2006.

Chusmir, L. and Mills, J. "Gender differences in conflict resolution styles of managers: At work and at home." *Sex Roles* 20, 1989, 149-63.

Crabb, Larry. *Men and Women.* Grand Rapids, MI: Zondervan, 1993.

Devine, P. G. "Stereotypes and prejudice: Their automatic and controlled components." *Journal of Personality and Social Psychology* 56, 1989, 5-18.

De Wall, Frans B.M. "The end of nature versus nurture." *Scientific American,* December 1999.

Dowling, Colette. *The Frailty Myth.* New York: Random House, 2000.

Doyle, James A., and Paludi, Michelle A. *Sex and Gender: The Human Experience.* Boston: McGraw-Hill, 1998.

Fausto-Sterling, A. *Myths of Gender: Biological Theories About Men and Women.* New York: Basic Books, 1992.

Folger, J. P., M. S. Poole, and R. K. Stutman. *Working Through Conflict: Strategies for Relationships, Groups, and Organizations,* 3rd ed. New York: Addison-Wesley, 1997.

Gaulin, Steven J. C. "How and why sex differences evolve, with spatial ability as a paradigm example." *The Development of Sex Differences and Similarities in Behavior,* ed. M. Haug. Netherlands: Kluwer Academic Publishers, 1993.

Gobi, A., and Moore, D. "Role Conflict and Perceptions of Gender Roles." *A Journal of Research* 32, 1995.

Gray, John. *Mars and Venus in the Bedroom: A Guide to Lasting Romance and Passion.* New York: HarperCollins, 2001.

————. *Mars and Venus in the Workplace: A Practical Guide for Improving Communication and Getting Results at Work.* New York: HarperCollins, 2001.

————. *Men Are from Mars, Women Are from Venus: A Practical Guide for Improving Communication and Getting What You Want in Your Relationships.* New York: HarperCollins, 1993.

————.*Why Mars and Venus Collide: Improving Relationships by Understanding How Men and Women Cope Differently with Stress.* New York: HarperCollins, 2008.

Greenleaf, R.K. *Servant Leadership: A Journey Into the Nature of Legitimate Power and Greatness.* NY: Paulist Press, 1983.

Griffith, Carol. "Personality and gender as factors in interpersonal negotiation." *Journal of Social and Behavior Personality* 6, 1991, 915-28.

Gupta, V., Turban, D., Wasti, S., and Sikdar, A. "Entrepreneurship and stereotypes: Are entrepreneurs from Mars or from Venus?" K. M. Weaver, ed., *Academy of Management Best Paper Proceedings* [CD ROM]. Honolulu, HI: Academy of Management, 2005.

Harris, Judith Rich. *The Nurture Assumption.* New York: Touchstone, 1998.

Heen, Sheila. "Defining gender differences: Is the proof in the process?" *Negotiation Journal* 12, 1996, 9-17.

Hines, M. *Brain Gender.* New York: Oxford University Press, 2005.

Holden, C. "Talk about a gender stereotype." *Science Now* 503, 2007.

House, R., Hanges, P., Javidan, M., Dorfman, P., and Gupta, V. *Culture, Leadership, and Organizations: The GLOBE Study of 62 Societies.* Sage Publications, 2004.

Hoyenga, Katharine Blick, and Kermit T. Hoyenga. *Gender Related Differences: Origins and Outcomes.* Boston: Allyn and Bacon, 1993.

James, Deborah, and Janice Drakich. "Understanding gender differences in amount of talk." *Gender and Conversational Interaction*, ed. Deborah Tannen. Oxford: Oxford University Press, 1993.

Kennedy, C. "Gender differences in committee decision-making: Process and outputs in an experimental setting." *Women & Politics* 25, no. 3, 2003, 27-45.

Klenke, K. "Gender influences in decision-making processes in top management teams." *Management Decision* 41, no. 10, 2003, 1024.

Kray, L. J., Thompson, L., and Galinsky, A. "Battle of the sexes: Gender stereotype confirmation and reactance in negotiations." *Journal of Personality and Social Psychology* 80, 2001, 942-58.

Lauzen, M., Dozier, D., and Horan, N. June. "Constructing gender stereotypes through social roles in prime-time television." *Journal of Broadcasting & Electronic Media* 52, no. 2, 2008, 200-14.

Lips, Hilary M. *Sex and Gender.* Mountain View, CA: Mayfield Publishing, 2001.

Luhaorg, H., and Zivian, M. T. "Gender Role Conflict: The Interaction of Gender, Gender Role, and Occupation." *Sex Roles: A Research Journal,* 1995.

Maccoby, Eleanor E. *The Two Sexes.* Cambridge, MA: Belknap Press, 1998.

Merrill, David W.; and Reid, Roger H. *Personal Styles and Effective Performance.* Radnor, PA: Chilton Book Co., 1981.

Moir, Anne, and Jessel, David. *Brain Sex: The Real Difference Between Men and Women.* New York: Delta, 1989.

————. and Bill Moir. *Why Men Don't Iron.* New York. Citadel Press, 1999.

Nevid, Jeffrey S. "Sex differences in factors of romantic attraction." *Sex Roles* 11, no. 5/6, 1984.

Norfleet, Abigail. *Teaching the Male Brain: How Boys Think, Feel, and Learn in School.* Thousand Oaks, CA: Corwin Press, 2007.

Parke, Ross D., and Brott, Armin A. *Throwaway Dads: The Myths and Barriers That Keep Men from Being the Fathers They Want to Be.* Boston: Houghton Mifflin, 1999.

Phillips, Bob. *Controlling Your Emotions Before They Control You.* Eugene, OR: Harvest House, 1995.

————. *The Delicate Art of Dancing with Porcupines.* Ventura, CA: Regal Books, 1989.

"Reality Check: The Gender Revolution." *Washington Post,* 22 March, 1998.

Sax, Leonard. *Why Gender Matters: What Parents and Teachers Need to Know About the Emerging Science of Sex Differences.* New York: Broadway, 2006.

————. *Boys Adrift: The Five Factors Driving the Growing Epidemic of Unmotivated Boys and Underachieving Young Men.* New York: Basic Books, 2007.

Smetzer, Larry R. and Watson, Kittie W. "Gender differences in verbal communication during negotiations." *Communication Research Reports* 3, 1986, 74-79.

Steele, C.M. "A threat in the air: How stereotypes shape intellectual identity and performance." *American Psychologist* 52, 1997, 613-29.

Tannen, Deborah. *You Just Don't Understand: Women and Men in Conversation.* New York: William Morrow, 1990.

Townsend, John Marshall. *What Women Want—What Men Want.* New York: Oxford University Press, 1998.

Walsh, Mary Roth. *Women, Men, and Gender: Ongoing Debates.* New Haven: Yale University Press, 1997.

Wegener, D.T., Clark, J.K., and Petty, R.E. "Not all stereotyping is created equal: Differential consequences of thoughtful versus nonthoughtful stereotyping." *Journal of Personality and Social Psychology* 90, no. 1, 2006, 42-59.

White, M., and White, G. Aug. "Implicit and explicit occupational gender stereotypes." *Sex Roles* 55, no. 3/4, 2006, 259-66.

About the Authors

Kimberly Alyn is a human behavior expert, an international speaker, and a bestselling author. She has been studying human behavior for more than 20 years and travels the world educating and entertaining audiences, helping people grow personally and professionally. Kim speaks to corporate, municipal, association, and church audiences on various topics such as overcoming gender myths, dealing with annoying people, rising to effective leadership, applying principles of successful living, and giving dynamic presentations.

800-821-8116
Kim@KimberlyAlyn.com
www.KimberlyAlyn.com
www.MenAreSlobsWomenAreNeat.com
www.HowToDealWithAnnoyingPeople.com

Bob Phillips is a New York Times bestselling author and holds a Ph.D. in counseling. He is a licensed marriage and family therapist in California. He is also a founding director of the Pointman Leadership Institute. Bob has presented seminars on ethics and the importance of character in leadership in 20 countries.

Bob has written more than 100 books with more than ten million copies in print. When not speaking or writing, Bob can be found mountain climbing, cave exploring, motorcycle riding, or enjoying his most important interests: his wife of 43 years, his two daughters and sons-in laws, and his three grandsons.

bob2hume@aol.com

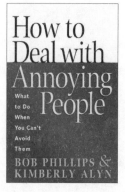

How to Deal with Annoying People
Kimberly Alyn and Bob Phillips

The world is filled with annoying people, but here is hope and help! This look at personality styles and close, sometimes conflicted interaction reveals why you are occasionally annoyed by others, why others are annoyed by you, and what you can do to create fantastic relationships.

You'll get along better in both professional and personal relationships as you employ biblical principles along with a fun and simple process of identifying social cues.

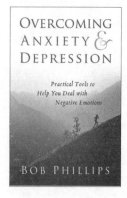

Overcoming Anxiety and Depression
Bob Phillips

You will readily identify with licensed family counselor Bob Phillips as he provides descriptions of the potentially debilitating effects of anxiety and depression. He reveals the root causes of anxiety and depression, which are fear and anger, and he helps you acknowledge and deal with these driving forces in an effective, godly way.

This hands-on, user-friendly approach is written with the lay person in mind and includes plenty of practical and effective self-help exercises that you can use to find freedom. Bob's system is built on a solid foundation of scriptural principles and up-to-date technical research on mental health.

To learn more about other Harvest House books
or to read sample chapters, log on to our website:

www.harvesthousepublishers.com

HARVEST HOUSE PUBLISHERS

EUGENE, OREGON